Tsunami'd by God

Healing of a Father-Wound

by Fr. Philip Scott F.J.

Copyright © 2025 by Fr. Philip Scott, F.J., Tampa, FL

All rights reserved. No part of this publication may be reproduced, distributed, or transmitted in any form or by any means, including photocopying, recording, or other electronic or mechanical methods, without the prior written permission of the author, except as permitted by U.S. copyright law.

ISBN – 9798282660661 (paperback – English)

It may be that any advice and/or guidance contained herein may not apply to you, or be suitable for your situation. If you think spiritual guidance would benefit you, you should seek spiritual advice from a source of your own choosing, but it is highly recommended that the person you choose be qualified or certified by an approved Roman Catholic Church entity.

Occasionally, material under copyright from other sources was incorporated into this book as quotations. Wherever used, it has been clearly cited, and bibliographical information is included at the end of the book. The editor has ensured compliance with permissions guidance from applicable publishers.

Book Covers by Shelly Pichler

Editing by Anne Detten

First edition 2025

*If we want to receive the "tsunami" of Jesus' mercy that He is so very eager to give us,
then we must also give mercy to others.*

- the Author

Table of Contents

Endorsements iii
Acknowledgements viii
Author's Notes.. xv
Introduction 1
Chapter One – The Wound in the Heart of the Family: Absence of the "Blessing" in Family Life........................ 9
Chapter Two – My Own Childhood Experience, the Absence of the Blessing: The Father Wound 51
Chapter Three – "Get two handkerchiefs..." 58
Chapter Four – An Un-Parented Child turned Father Fathers with Many Difficulties.. 74
.... 86
Chapter Five – The Heart of a Child Who Has not Experienced the Blessing 95
Chapter Six – God Brings His Missing Blessing to the Un-fathered Wounded 106
Chapter Seven – God Fathers Us by First Weakening Us
.... 113
Chapter Eight – Jesus: The Only Son – to Whom Does He Reveal the Father? 128
Chapter Nine – My Encounter with the Father, My Papa
.... 146
Chapter Ten – Who You Really Are – A Life of Being Forgiven... 180

Epilogue 213
Appendices 217
   Some Words for Those Discerning Whether or Not to Have Children 219
   A Heart's Suffering through Its Personal Holy Week 228
   Even (Especially) When We Blow it Royally, God is Still Faithful 237
Bibliography 242
Biographical Summary – Father Philip Scott 247

Endorsements

Bishop Scott McCaig - Author's Bishop

Drawing from the deep wellspring of the Scriptures, sound spirituality and psychology, and his own experiences, Fr. Philip has produced a book on the Father's Blessing that is both rich in insight and deeply healing when applied to our own lives. I recommend it for every disciple of Jesus yearning to grow in intimacy with our loving Father.

+Bishop Scott McCaig, C.C.
Military Ordinary of Canada

"+Bishop McCaig was…appointed [in 2016] by Pope Francis to be the Bishop of the Military Ordinariate of Canada, which serves the varied spiritual and pastoral needs of [Canadian] military members and their families.

"+Bishop Scott serves on the Board of Renewal Ministries Canada and has participated in missionary outreach to over 15 countries in Africa, Eastern Europe, and Southeast Asia….and is author of 'Clothed with Power from On High: A Short Catechesis on Charisms in the Life and Mission of the Church."

Information taken from Bishop McCaig's diocesan website
https://rcmilord-ordmilcr.com/offices

Cynthia Hunt MD

"Tsunami'd by God" is a remarkable writing! This book could easily have been titled "A Retreat with Father Philip." As I read it, there were multiple times when I was moved to pause, ponder and reflect on its contents – in a manner similar to Lectio Divina. I found that I was not able to 'read' it as a typical book.

Father is very real and down-to-earth in his presentation. He doesn't claim to be a professional in his guidance with woundedness, but through his testimony and deep prayer life, he gives us significant insights into interior healing.

It is clear that his wisdom and experience inform his writing. I highly recommend this book and the blessings which accompany it.

Cynthia Hunt MD

Dr. Cynthia Hunt serves as Director of Holy Alliance Support Ministry/Psychiatrist Consultant, and is Board Certified in Internal Medicine, Pediatrics and Psychiatry. She is currently a Faculty Member of St. Patrick's Seminary and University and also served as Chief of Psychiatry for three years at the Community Hospital of the Monterey Peninsula. In addition, Dr. Hunt served the Catholic Medical Association (CMA) as board member and a frequent speaker. She was Chair of the National CMA Opioid Task Force which met regularly from 2018 to 2020 with US Department of Health and Human Services, earning a "Lifetime Achievement Award in Catholic Healthcare" in 2019 for her work with the opioid crisis.

Dr. Rosa María Normand Fort

Father Phillip's book describes powerful images of his own personal experience, and unites them with Bible texts and enlightening reflections – teaching the reader and motivating us to follow that path that takes us from our personal wounds to the healing and fulfilling experience of becoming fathered by God the Father.

Father Phillip guides us along the narrow path which takes us from the pain of several forms of being unloved by significant persons in our life, to experiencing the joy of being parented and loved by the Divine LOVE. Reading his book awakens new and strong hopes of the real possibility of that fulfilling Union with God The Father. Union for which we are all longing from the deepest areas of our hearts. He shows us, in a very close and vivid way, how we can transit from our personal cross, our wounds, to the resurrection of a new life in perfect union with God. Union that gives us peace, joy, meaning and self-knowledge, that is above our highest expectations.

Thank you, Father Phillip, for sharing your experiences in a so honest, profound, enriching and genuine way, so that we, by reading your book, receive nurturing to grow our hopes of reaching the life-giving union with our God.

Dr. Rosa María Normand Fort

Dr. Normand Fort is a highly regarded psychoanalyst in Lima Peru. She is a published author in respected journals, to include Revista de Psicología, in which her article concerning research and work with abandoned and orphaned children appeared. Dr. Normand Fort has been associated with the Pontifical Catholic University of Peru.

Acknowledgements

Thank You!

I would like to thank my community – The Family of Jesus – for having been the place where I have most learned about family life. You have been so patient with me. I love all of you deeply!

I would also like to thank from the bottom of my heart:

My Eternal Family (Father, Son and Holy Spirit): You are my All! I call You my "TODO." Thank you for adopting me into THE FAMILY in baptism. Your love has left me speechless and almost made me die of love. I dedicate this book to YOU – Father, Son, and Holy Spirit! May I one day love You "to death" and find myself with You forever my Home and with the Communion of Saints!

My twin Fr. Martin Scott (my Riñon[1]): We were "womb-mates" and have walked together on our healing journey. Thank you for your child-like faith, purity of heart, and example of spending yourself for God and the poor through your priesthood. You have been a beautiful

---

[1] Literal translation into English = Kidney. I use Riñon here as a colloquialism – and mean by this word that my twin is inseparable from my life.

witness and spiritual Father to your own community (Servants of Divine Mercy), and the poorest of the poor. Let us persevere my dear "Riñon." When mom took off the gas mask it was God 's intervention, so let us be generous unto death for this life to learn to *love* so to be forever living in our Family (the Trinity), with the family. I love you deeply!

Your "Monito" [2]

Aunt Tula (Tia Tula): You have been a living example of a life of faith as a Catholic; though we lovingly called you "inspector of base boards" because of your height – you are a giant in the family! O Tia Tula, how I love you and thank you for mothering me and how I laugh at the memories of you telling me of being a champion (campeona). You always noticed the "weather report" in my heart. You really <u>saw</u> and <u>heard</u> me, your nephews, nieces and so many that met you. Tia Tula - there is only one Tia Tula! I so love you!

Your "Philiberto"

Lorraine Scott: We have talked much. I thank you for the example of your womanhood and motherhood. You have responded to grace and healed much. Continue on my dear sister. You have loved and loved well. Whenever I give a retreat and you are there, I feel you are in my

---

[2] Translates into English as "little monkey."

corner and cheering me on, like only a sister could do. I love you!

Your brother

Margie Enders (my other sister): I remember being little and playing "school." You were my teacher. I think it is the only time I did well in school! I thank you for so often allowing your home to be a place for my heart to rest. I thank you and Bob for that. I am so welcomed there. I love you!

Your brother

Mike Fuller: My dear Mike! You are a brother of my soul; a friend for all my priesthood and a man dedicated to his wife, children and Church. You are <u>blessed</u> and a close friend of Our Lord, for you have suffered well for Him. Like Him you have been taking to the cross in so many ways. I love you, Sandy and the children.

Father

Since I originally wrote this thank you to my soul brother Mike, he has died, and is now Home with God, our Father.

Gaetano and Pilar Garibaldi: I will never forget our first meeting as I was beginning the Hispanic community at St. Paul's in Tampa. For your friendship, love, support of the community and for me, I am so grateful. Thank you for your longing to be faithful to God at whatever the cost. I love you!

Felipe

Dr. Tom Byron: You are now home where we will one day see one another after my mission is complete here. You did well in being a father figure for me. I love you, Tom!

God's "ELITE" - "mis hijos de Vallecito" ³: Only in eternity will you know how I love you and how hard I cried to have to leave you when we moved to Puerto Maldonado. I was given "eyes" and "ears" in a new way when our lives crossed. Thank you for being you, mis "hijitos" of my soul. I will be forever "Padre." I will forever love to hear all of you say to me, "Padre." Thank you for teaching me so much! Los quiero muchisimo!

Padre

Anne Detten: Thank you, Anne, for your patience and kindness in editing this book. You were for me more than an editor but also an instrument sent from God to encourage me to not give up on this project and to persevere. Your insight and kind prayerfulness are so appreciated by me and Our Lord!

Shelly Pichler: Shelly, I have told you often that you are for me the sister I wished I could have had. What a gift you are! How often you have welcomed me into your

---

³ Translated, this means "my sons of Vallecito."

home, and your heart, along with Eric, your good and holy husband. Thank you for your love, prayers and insights and continual encouragement. Eric and you are, for me, family!!!

Dad and Mom,
You are now Home. If I had you together in front of me, I would tell you, "All has turned out well." Dad, I once had an interesting experience with you: I was on retreat, and suddenly I felt as if you were with me and the words came to my heart, "I now love you without wounds." Those words touched me deeply. I know you do and I always believed you did, but your own wounds were too strong and you never sought to heal them on this side of eternity. I did not turn out that bad and God, who is so good and GOODNESS itself, has used all for His plan and for His glory. I thank you for loving Mom so well and giving me an example on how a man should protect and love his wife. You did that well. You also were an honest and hard-working man. You were a generous man with the poor. I also want to thank you for telling me, when I told you I was no longer a Catholic but a "Christian" for your answer – "If you live under my roof, you must go to Mass. If you want to go to another church, you can do so when you can support yourself and move out." All is well, very well. And Mom, we were able to talk quite a bit, as we examined your life while you were still alive on earth. We will one day rejoice and laugh together that God was

bigger and much greater than all our sins, mistakes and human frailty. Glory to God! He Alone suffices!

Your Philip

Author's Notes

Biblical quotes are from the New American Bible (NAB), except where otherwise noted, or when the Bible quote appears within quoted material.

Also, please carefully note the bibliographical information for quoted works, to include the edition number of the work and whether quoted work is hardcover or paperback edition.

Introduction

After being asked for years by men, women and even children, "So Father, when am I going to read your book?" I decided to take a stab at writing a book. The last nudge I needed to get me started on this work came from a Catholic psychologist on the west coast of the United States, who attended one of my retreats.

I have never considered myself a writer. God seems to think otherwise.

What else is new? Jeremiah told God he was too young; and Moses told God he could not speak. So, I am in incredibly good company at trying to convince God with an attitude of "You cannot mean me?" And here you have it – the book which I have been asked to write for years.

You have in your hands a book that is my humble reflection on one of the deepest wounds in the hearts of men and women, rich and poor, the ordained clergy and the laity, the believer and the unbeliever – the "father wound." In my travels throughout the United States, Latin America, Korea and other countries, I have seen this wound in a very substantial number of people that have attended my retreats, in counseling, in "chance meetings" that seemed at first just a coincidence – when in fact they were God-incidences.

When my parents moved with their six children to the United States in 1965, we first landed in Miami. One day my father took us on a boat trip. Since I could not see, I was very afraid that we were going to sink. I must have been telling my father over and over again, "Are we going to sink?" Finally, he picked me up and let me see outside to what from my small vantage point as a child, I was unable to see before. Once I saw the bigger picture, I was at peace and could enjoy the boat ride.

When one is wounded, one does not really "see" life well. He or she cannot enjoy his journey of life. Indeed, my experience and those of many others who have shared their similar experiences with me, is that one's wounds are so "loud" or so large that the vantage point of life is obscured. Such people "see" through a lens clouded with fears, self-hatred, insecurity, shame and have built a wall around one's heart that is their way trying to be self-sufficient and strong. Life often is a battle of survival, of fighting against inner turmoil. One cannot see the beauty of God's plan.

Often, if God the Father's dream is experienced within one's heart at all, it plays more like a "nightmare."

In these pages I want to open my heart and share my own journey of healing from my own father wound. It is NOTHING like a three-hour movie that begins and then hours later ends with the words – THE END. Our hearts are mysterious with seasons, like the seasons of our year. And at first, we do not understand the various seasons found there. Yet we slowly grow to understand that this wound did not just appear overnight, so it will not heal overnight either.

It is here that we must experience a voice of hope. Hopefully, this voice comes from a man who becomes a "father figure" who has worked through his own issues and has seen the hand of God-the-Parent gently putting His fingers in this father figure's wounds. And equally hopefully, this father figure is a person who understands what is in his own heart and how God uses grace to help us overcome our fallen nature, becoming more like Him – in Whose image we were made after all.

We are, as Scriptures say in Jeremiah, clay in the Father's hands: "'Can I not do to you, ... as this potter has done?' says the LORD. Indeed, like clay in the hand of the potter, so are you in my hand...' (Jer 18:6) This clay must be turned over and over again by events that expose our brokenness. Likewise, this earth of our hearts must be turned over so our hearts will become fertile with each season of tears. Such a person is a wise man and has a special gift, if he begins to see that there is light that at first was hidden underneath his pain.

Fathers that work through their pain and sin, whether they be biological or spiritual fathers, are in demand and a rare breed. Such men begin to see life through a life of prayer and see heaven's vantage point in daily events for they know the Father is always near them. Such men are fathers who have experienced being parented by the Father of Jesus who is also our Father.

I was blessed to meet such a man, Dr. Tom Byron, as a young priest. You will hear of him in this book. I would like to let you peek into my heart. It was once a heart with a crater-size father wound. With time and after a strong conversion experience where my Lord Jesus became more real than life itself, I was slowly and gently taken deeply into my heart by the Divine Healer and Creator of our hearts. This process involved some counseling but mostly through the great "I AM" found in every tabernacle of every Catholic Church.

From my early years of adoration at St. Charles Borromeo College Seminary in Cleveland, Ohio, I began to truly experience that Jesus was in the tabernacle *for me*. This "I

AM" was now experienced as an "I AM here for you!" That is the Truth! In the pages that follow I want to share those intense prayer experiences with a God who understands us beyond our wildest dreams.

I was a young man who dated and was about to marry when God let me know that He had other plans. This healing of the father wound slowly began to instruct me on how to date. A good father is able to discuss with his son topics like dating and other important life issues. God is no different. My Papa (my name for God the Father) did that in a way that was very gentle but lovingly and brutally truthful. His standard was much higher than the version of purity I lived as a young man.

In God's dream for men, a true man is pure. Jesus states in the Beatitudes some eternal truths, such as "Blessed are the clean of heart, for they will see God." (Matt 5:8) I pray that you will see that any wound you have does not have the last word. The Father, the perfect Parent, wants you to know that His Son is His final word – a word of healing, mercy, truth and liberation.

In the upcoming pages I will share with you also my heart felt discovery of learning to love as a spiritual father - about "fathering" spiritual sons and daughters in an age where so many live in houses where they are not really noticed by their parents. The sons and daughters are not known by their parents. We live in times where more than ever we need men and women living the prophetic call of celibacy and chastity to be spiritual fathers and mothers to so many unparented souls that are the "walking wounded." May we see this sign of the times become reality today.

I will also discuss my initial encounter with my Papa and what it has been to be fathered by Him. My life has become a sharing of my daily events with my Father. It is no longer me facing every new challenge on my own, but He and me ("Us") together walking the "narrow" path. St. Paul writes in his letter to the Romans, "For all of you who were baptized into Christ have clothed yourselves with Christ." (Gal 3:27)

We, the baptized, are invited to taste and see from this side of *eternity* a glimpse of the life of Jesus as Son in *the very fiber* of our beings. Through your reading of this book, I hope you see a glimpse of how He has brought me and others to taste a bit of His life as Son. We, the baptized, are adopted into the Family of God and invited to live our deepest and truest identity as sons and daughters of the Father.

I wish I could just sit with you over a cup of coffee and just talk and help you listen to your own heart. This is not possible, so we must accept the medium of this book to assist in enabling God's work to be completed in us.

In writing about my parents, I hope to not dishonor them in any way. If anything, I wish to look at them and smile and tell them, "All has become good and useful in the Father's plan." I am grateful for all that God willed or allowed in His mysterious plan that at first was exceedingly difficult and painful. Like the title of a great Italian movie I can shout out, "Life is beautiful" even when it is filled with pain. Why?

Because as we progress in this process of healing, we begin to be more aware of a mysterious plan that God has begun and will bring to completion if we only allow Him to father us.

The book is written in a manner that appeals to our heads but leads us to our hearts. It is there that we will experience the "look" of unconditional love from the only Perfect Parent - the Father, my Papa. It is a book that is written with simplicity because God is so perfectly simple Himself, so much so that we can never wrap our understanding around Him.

Only to the "simple" – to the child-like is this mystery revealed even to any real degree, and Jesus praised His Father for this, "I give praise to you, Father, Lord of heaven and earth, for although you have hidden these things from the wise and the learned you have revealed them to the childlike.'" (Matt 11:25). Did not Philip say to Jesus in John's gospel, "Master, show us the Father, and that will be enough for us." (John 14:8).

So let us put ourselves into the hands of Our Blessed Mother Mary, who far more than any other creature knows the Father, because she knows Jesus - the Son. After all, Our Lord Himself promises us, "I will not leave you orphans" in John 14:18. And this verse continues, "I will come to you." So, let Jesus come to you. ASK Him to come close to you. Be not afraid!

He is the Divine Healer who reveals to us the Father's face. You who hold this book in your hands are called to be a saint - to live in the Sonship of Jesus. Be not afraid! You are the Father's.

Tampa, Florida
Feast of Our Lady of the Rosary 2022

Chapter One – The Wound in the Heart of the Family: Absence of the "Blessing" in Family Life

For a father's blessing gives a family firm roots, but a mother's curse uproots the growing plant. (Sirach 3:9)

The Human Heart is Delicate and Created for the Blessing of God the Father through the Parents

When I was seven years old my neighbor who was of the same age came to me and said her father was going to build us an airplane. He was going to use two lawn mower engines to make the two new engines for the airplane. She told me, "You can be the pilot and I will be the flight attendant." Nothing could convince me that in a few weeks we would not be flying our own new airline.

This event in my childhood has reminded me of the purity and innocence of the heart of a child; and that memory has helped me to remain in touch with the world of a child. Children are meant to dream and dream big. They look for heroes to imitate. They dream of flying, of running faster than anyone in the world. Their lives are full of possibilities. The "sky and beyond" is their limit. Home needs to be a place where such dreams are expressed. Children have so much to discover.

Life at home needs to be a place where it is safe to feel, imagine and to express what is felt and imagined and where there is much laughter and joy. This memory in my past invites me to enter into the mystery of our Lord's words in Mathew's Gospel, "Amen, I say to you, unless you turn and become like children, you will not enter the kingdom of heaven. Whoever humbles himself like this child is the greatest in the kingdom of heaven." (Matt 18:3-4) We adults need to let ourselves be formed into children of God and in this process be healed of any de-formation that we experienced in our homes and exile from our true home - heaven.

Yes, through our Baptism, we are sons and daughters of the Father, but to learn and be re-formed in a filial relationship with the Father takes a lifetime of docility to the Spirit's promptings, fidelity to a life of prayer and seeking and doing His will and a donation of ourselves that often includes suffering. It is a process that leads to what St. Paul called the "freedom" of the children of God (see Rom 8:21). With the increase of the divorce rate, one parent households and work schedules that are too long, children often find themselves alone and raising themselves.

Sadly, these one-parent homes often have a parent that truly must work hard to make ends meet. The parent must become the "super-mom" or "super-dad." These parents are truly heroic in what they strive to do for their children. However, even in the best of non-ideal circumstances, the children can often be left to fend for themselves. They become "game" for older kids and adults who themselves are so wounded that they look for their next victim in whatever shape or form the victim comes.

Such children feel unimportant and do not have a healthy self-image, so they must invent their identity because they do not have a parent actively involved in forming them in love and truth. Often these parents cannot connect emotionally with their children because they themselves never connected emotionally with their own parents. There is great anguish in their own hearts.

Too many parents come out of childhoods where they themselves were not formed by a healthy parent-child relationship. They never truly had a good parent-son or parent-daughter relationship. They lacked from their parents what the Scriptures call the blessing. *(Hereinafter referred to as the "Blessing" throughout this book.)*

The *Catechism of the Catholic Church* states, "The divine fatherhood is the source of human fatherhood; this is the foundation of the honor owed to parents." (CCC 2214) The Scriptures speak of the Blessing as a way, a daily experience of home life, of a relationship between a son and a daughter with their parents. Sirach 3:9 tells us something about the Blessing between son and daughter and their parents, and of what a blessing means for a family. We read, "For a father's blessing gives a family firm roots, but a mother's curse uproots the growing plant."

The idea of blessing can be the foundation for family life. I am grateful to the authors of a book called *The Blessing* for their insight and experience. The Old Testament concept of the Blessing is beautifully developed in this book by Christian therapists John Trent, Ph.D. and Dr. Gary Smalley, both Christians and fathers. The idea of the Blessing as the foundation of family life to be handed down from generation to generation is found in the Old Testament. In my treatment of this Old Testament concept as described in this work, I have changed the last and fifth part of the Blessing from "an active commitment to fulfill the blessing" to "Loving parental correction/discipline."

The concept of the Blessing best describes and confirms what I believe has been the foundation for family life in my working with families for over three decades as a priest. Let us jump into this wisdom that comes from no other than God as found in the pages of the Bible. I have changed the wording of each part of the Blessing, but the general idea comes from this wonderful book (cited above).

So, what is "the Blessing?" It has five aspects:

1. Meaningful touch.
2. Words spoken that are constructive, affirmative and life-giving.

3. A child experiences having a unique worth in the eyes of his parents.

4. Parents form a positive and empowering image of the future of their children.

5. Parental correction and discipline springs from love. This in turn leads to an experience of forgiveness, unconditional love and deeper bonding through a deeper interpersonal encounter with a father and a mother. It is also a reflection of the way God at times treats us as sons and daughters. (Please

read Heb 12:5-11 for a beautiful description of how God disciplines His children.)

1. Meaningful touch:

"For children, things become real when they are touched." [4]

The body has been described as an "extension" of the soul. Doctors John Trent and Gary Smalley write in their book *The Blessing*, "Parents in particular need to know that neglecting to meaningfully touch their children starves them of genuine acceptance - so much so that it can drive them to the arms of someone else who is all too willing to touch them." [5]

When I first arrived in Peru as a missionary in 2003, I was surprised to see how many children in the slum where we ministered wanted to be held, stroked during Mass and outside of Mass. I would preside at Mass and children would come up to me and just lean their little head on my shoulder. In Peru I have been told by a priest friend of mine who is a psychologist that 65% of the babies born in Peru are abandoned by their fathers before they are born. I know a woman who was born in a family where affection

---

[4] Page 50, Trent, J and Smalley G. *The Blessing*.
[5] Ibid. Page 48.

was rarely, if ever, expressed by her parents, and she would hold herself in bed so at least at some point in her day she would feel a human touch.

In the Old Testament when a parent or grandfather would impart the blessing, he would lovingly touch the child or grandchild. We read of Jacob (Israel) doing this when he met Joseph's children for the first time.

When Joseph brought his sons close to Israel, Israel kissed the sons, and said

> *"Bring them to me...that I may bless them." Now Israel's eyes were dim from age, and he could not see well. When Joseph brought his sons close to him, he kissed and embraced them."* (Gen 48:9-10) (Italics mine.)

Pay attention to how Jacob embraces and kisses Joseph's children one by one. If we did not receive this loving touch, we would look for it. The loving touch is soothing to a child's body. The body and heart relax. How many times have we seen children just "laying" on the parent's lap, looking into the sky and playing with their parent's hands? The child is totally relaxed because he is receiving God's touch through the parent, feeling safe and loved.

The child receives a Blessing through their parents' loving touches. When I was a newly ordained priest, a relative, who was seven years old, wanted her mother to brush her hair. I told my young relative, "I will brush your hair." As I brushed her hair, I played with her little ears and kissed her head. The little girl giggled and laughed. To this day she remembers the place and day I brushed her hair. It was not that I was a hair stylist. (I can barely comb my own hair.) It was that she experienced a loving touch. It made her day.

Jesus, creator of all children, did no less for we read in Luke's gospel, "People were bringing even infants to him that he might touch them ..." (Luke 18:15). He even rebuked his disciples for not allowing the children to come to him. And then we read in Mark's gospel that Jesus took the children into his arms, "Then he embraced them and blessed them, placing his hands on them." (Mark 10:16)

You who are reading these words had an innate need to be held, touched lovingly by your father and mother. To have received it has prepared you to impart this aspect of the Blessing to your children and family and friends. To have not received this part of the Blessing is to live with anguish – a cry in your soul to really know you have a unique worth and are irreplaceable.

The loving touch forms us; it touches a part of our being that brings a security and a sense of "I am loved and lovable' to a child. A loving touch can quiet a crying child. To be touched is to feel "home" – it gives security and a place of belonging – in the place called the heart, a refuge. The world could fall apart, but for a son or daughter who is in their parents' arms – all is well!

I am reminded of the Italian film, "Life is Beautiful." The setting of the film is during the Nazi occupation of Italy, and the story is about the relationship of a beautiful family whose father is deeply in love with his wife, his princess. They have a son who is protected by the love, playfulness and affection of his father. This type of fathering so soothes, and protects the son from the trauma of the Nazi occupation, that even when the entire family is taken into one of the concentration camps, the father insists on teaching the son a game.

Amid the horror of the concentration camp, the son's heart is nurtured, loved, fed and instructed by the father even when the father is being taken to be executed. He marches off as a "soldier" with a smile and a wink of an eye. The son is held by the gaze and captivating fatherly love of his father. Life was shown to be truly "beautiful" despite living Nazi mistreatment. When the child is protected, he is safe… he is "home."

This refuge called "home" is not just a place with walls but the place of the heart of the parents. Here their children grow up, and develop and discover their identity and eventually their "calling" to be in service of the Eternal Parent, God the Father.

2. Words spoken that are constructive, affirmative and life-giving:

We are told in Scripture that our tongue can impart a blessing or a curse. We read in the letter of James,

> "In the same way the tongue is a small member and yet has great pretensions. Consider how small a fire can set a huge forest ablaze. The tongue is also a fire. It exists among our members as a world of malice, defiling the whole body and setting the entire course of our lives on fire, itself set on fire by Gehenna." (James 3:5-6)

I remember leading a group of men in a men's group who were poor and I asked them, "How many of you experienced words of affirmation?" They looked at me with faces and an expression that communicated, "What are you talking about?" They understood Spanish but did not know the power of words of affirmation in their lives.

Their faces showed little expression. Their eyes communicated the need to cry but the sad reality that they were never given the opportunity to share their years of being wounded by painful *words*.

The Jewish people had a saying that to be cursed by painful words is to slowly have your blood spilt. It is like slowly being put to death on an emotional level. How many people have grown up with words spoken to them that to this day "cut" their hearts? In sessions of counseling and spiritual direction I have heard so many people who for the first time are able to share painful memories of hearing words that cut them to shreds.

For the one sharing his story the memory is fresh; it is happening to him as he speaks. This we call the curse – words that wound destroy the human spirit instead of forming it or building it up. Yet words can also breathe life into a person. This is powerfully expressed in the book of the prophet Ezekiel. We read in chapter 37:

> "The hand of the LORD came upon me, and he led me out in the spirit of the LORD and set me in the center of the plain, which was now filled with bones. He made me walk among them in every direction so that I saw how many they were on the surface of the plain. How dry they were!" (Ezek 37: 1-2)

Ezekiel sees a plain of dead dry bones that symbolizes the state of Israel and her army. She was slain and lifeless. Her "blood" had been spilt. *How many of us may feel lifeless because of painful words spoken to us?*

I met a beautiful woman in Latin America who told me she felt like trash, destroyed by a life of hearing words that were destructive and not a blessing. But wait – in the very next verse, God asked Ezekiel a question, "... Son of man, can these bones come to life?" (Ezek 37:3)

Our painful experience cannot have the last word. Jesus said, "the truth will set you free." (John 8:32). Our Lord also said, "I am the way and the truth and the life." (John 14:6) During his life, Ezekiel saw what words that came from the mouth of God; what words breathed by the very breath of the Eternal Father can do. Ezekiel was told by the Eternal Parent,

> "Then he said to me: Prophesy over these bones, and say to them: Dry bones, hear the word of the LORD! Thus says the Lord GOD to these bones: "See, I will bring spirit into you, that you may come to life. I will put sinews upon you, make flesh grow over you, cover you with skin, and put spirit in you so that you may come to life and know that I am

> the LORD. I prophesied as I had been told, and even as I was prophesying, I heard a noise; it was a rattling as the bones came together, bone joining bone. I saw the sinews and the flesh come upon them, and the skin cover them, but there was no spirit in them. Then he said to me: Prophesy to the spirit, prophesy, son of man, and say to the spirit: Thus says the Lord GOD: From the four winds come, O spirit, and breathe into these slain that they may come to life." (Ezek 37:4-9)

Ezekiel tasted, experienced what words spoken with love, authority – the very authority that come from the Eternal Parent – can do. Literally these words are capable of bringing people back to life! Life was breathed back into God's people, His chosen people. We will discuss later how God, the Eternal Parent, breathes life into those areas of our lives that have not experienced or tasted the Blessing. So loving words, words that come from the heart of THE Parent of parents, can restore life.

How often we have thought, "I will tell them 'I love you' tomorrow." When I feel God is asking me to say something to someone, I first say to myself, "You might never see them again." This leads me to say what I must say. The book of Proverbs has some advice, "Refuse no one the good on which he has a claim when it is in your power to do it for him. Say not to your neighbor, 'Go, and come again, tomorrow I will give,' when you can give at once." (Prov 3:27- 28)

3. A child experiences having a unique worth in the eyes of his parents.

One begins to experience and see this goodness when he is seen, noticed in a unique way. The way one is seen can transform a person. We read earlier that Jacob, when giving his Blessing to Joseph's children "saw" them. To be seen is more an experience of the heart than of the eyes. In a Spanish translation (Dios Habla Hoy) it says, "De pronto Israel (Jacob) se fijò en los hijos de Jose..." (Gen 48:8). He more than noticed them. Joseph FOCUSED on them; he saw them with more than his eyes. It implies a looking that is "fixed" on them. When we are noticed – when we are seen – in this way not only do eyes meet but so do souls. I like to say when one notices someone, they notice what "season" is in the heart of the person. One is truly seen and heard, and without having said a word one is *known*.

How about you, my dear reader? Were you ever noticed through someone's heart? Did you ever look into your parents' eyes and see their delight; their awe as their eyes filled with tears as they truly "saw" you? They're only you! To meet the eyes of a loving parent that is moved to tears is to sense the "gaze" of the Father. It is to enter a home, your home. Home must be more than an address on a street. It is a place where eyes meet; where a son and daughter taste the love, delight, unique place of their worth in their father's and mother's eyes – and where children and parents experience heart-moving and heart-changing encounters that transform their lives.

How else does one know their special, unique worth?

Children spell love – T – I – M – E. This means having parents spend time with us, quality time that creates beautiful memories. As a result, we develop a sense of being our parents' son or daughter unconditionally. This is more than just watching a ball game (this too is beautiful) or TV together.

It is a time where we discovered truth with our parents - about us, about a daily experience, about God's closeness in our life. It is a finding. It is a discovering, a being shown something beyond our vantagepoint. It is a small "wow" experience. In this "wow," there is for a moment a mysterious silence because our hearts know more than our minds – a moment that is an instant of time mixed with eternity.

I believe those "wow" experiences are Divine visitations disguised by the ordinary events of our encounters with others. Often such moments touch chords in our souls and spirits that are difficult to put into words because they come from the WORD made flesh who is SON from all eternity. These moments are sacred, for OUR PARENT is Fathering both parent and child in such moments.

For both parent and child are, in this instant, a son or daughter in the SON Our Eternal Parent.[6] This SON, who St. Thomas Aquinas called "pure act," is doing something in time, a something for which all involved must listen, reflect and work to see it from God's vantagepoint. For the Spirit is always about bringing God's will and work "on earth as it is in heaven." He is never "about" to do something. He never ceases. He is always doing, for Scripture tells us in Isaiah 55:11,

> "So shall my word be that goes forth from my mouth; it shall not return unto me void, but shall do my will, achieving the end for which I sent it."

His very essence is Love (1 Jn 4:8, 16), and He never ceases to love us.

---

[6] For some clarification - God Parents us in and through His Son. The Father is loving us always through His Son, the Word made flesh, our Lord Jesus Christ.

Both parent and child see something, Someone they could not see before – Someone in front of them who is a mystery to be discovered. Both parent and child "see" but now discover what is beyond what only "eyes" can see. They are shown something new. This new seeing comes from the Holy Spirit, and more happens than we might understand in such moments. They truly are a blessing!

I have often left such moments saying to those with whom I am in intimate conversation, "I believe we were not the only ones present during our conversation. Heaven was involved." All involved felt a mysterious pause, a real presence of Someone in their hearts. In 1John 4:16, we are told "We have come to know and believe in the love God has for us. God is Love, and whoever remains in love remains in God and God in Him!" In Acts 17:28 we read, "For 'in him we live and move and have our being." What a beautiful experience to know that we are "in God!"

When I walk, do counseling, wait in line, etc., I must recall that Jesus is very near. I believe this is what Brother Lawrence spoke about in his classic book *The Practice of the Presence of God* – that each and every moment can be lived in the presence of the Lord for He is already there with us, for He IS Emmanuel. This very moment, you whom I call God's favorite, are reading these pages. You with Him and He with you. It is an "Us" doing, reading and being.

A memory comes to mind that proves this point. Years ago, I was in the Philadelphia Airport, and there had just been a terrible snowstorm. The scene in the airport was, at best, chaotic – stranded passengers were screaming and arguing with employees of the airline. I remember realizing I was not alone. It was not just me in line. It was "We," Jesus and I were stranded in the airport. I gave my fiat, accepting the state of affairs, and thought that Eternity is about a hidden work and that He is aware of all this. Peace filled me. It was a moment as if God was truly seeing me.

Yes, He was there amidst all the screaming. I remembered the words of Hagar in Genesis 16:13 (RSV), "Thou art a God of seeing." He was close. He is close to you, my dear reader, even though you might be struggling.

Yet now, as you stare at these words stop and say, "You are with me." Share this with Him, your Eternal Parent. What do you sense? Might it be that He is approaching you, so dear to Him? Let Him find you – now. This might be a "wow!" moment. Ask Him for more, for He never tires of giving Himself. This moment is a discovery of reality.

And God IS reality.

What was going on around me during the chaos in the airport was not the ultimate reality. Your God and my God was and is about a work at this very moment and in those moments in the airport. A gentleman then asked me which religious community I belonged to. (My community wears a religious habit so we look like twelfth-century monks in a twenty-first century world.) He told me he was a Catholic but not an active Catholic. I thought to myself at first, "Here comes some anti-Catholic remarks." He was respectful. The man was a scientist and an atheist of Italian American descent. I asked for help because I had realized that I was not alone. It was God and me waiting in line. It was Jesus and me looking at this self-described "atheist."

I asked for inspiration from the Holy Spirit. Then I told the Italian atheist how much I enjoyed Italian food. He laughed and agreed as he described some dishes he enjoys cooking. We were standing in an extraordinarily long line that seemed to have an end (right where I was standing) but no beginning. I was tired, hungry and had an emergency in my system crying out for "bathroom." I think you get the picture. The gentleman was describing to me his favorite Italian dishes. So, I was now listening to an Italian menu being described. I told Jesus, "You are Italian," and I gently laughed.

Eventually we changed the topic from Italian food to whether God really existed and, if he did exist, why was He allowing such an uncomfortable moment in the lives of so many of His children? I told my new friend that God was at work even though we were not aware of it. The conversation, I realized at some point in the discussion, was one of the reasons that I was in this predicament. God is close, and eternity is mixing with our moments.

I tried every argument I knew to prove the existence of God including St. Thomas Aquinas' proof of the existence of God [7] and C.S. Lewis' proof for the existence of God [8]. The gentleman was not convinced.

We were slowly moving closer to the ticket counter and time was running out for us to catch the next and last flight out of Philadelphia. He asked me, "Does God care that you might have to spend two or three days in an airport since you are about to miss the only remaining flight?" I turned within my soul and sensed these words, "Fear not. You will be on the flight." I told him I was at peace and that God was in control; and that I would be on the flight.

---

[7] These proofs, five in all, are part of Aquinas' famous work *Summa Theologica*, but can now be found in many stand-alone publications,

[8] See Lewis' well-known work *Mere Christianity* for his discussion of this proof in detail.

I could not tell him that the Holy Spirit had just spoken in my heart.

Meanwhile, the American Airline employee was doing his best to get the other passengers in front of us on the last flight. One by one argued with him. I prayed for this poor man who was also tired and doing his best to help us. Again, I sensed a Peace come upon me. It was really an "Us" experience – me and Jesus. However, externally all seemed hopeless. The plane was about to leave and I could overhear the airline employee tell the passengers that we probably would not leave for two or three days since flights were so backed up and so many flights had been canceled. The phone rang at the counter. The employee picked up the phone and, before he heard a single word the caller was going to say, the employee muttered to himself, "I got bad news."

Again, I turned inward to Jesus, sensing an intense peace and I held on to the fact that Jesus is the reality; that He was with me and that all was well. I was suddenly called forward and the airline employee asked me my final destination. I was able to get on the flight. As I was leaving with my bags to give them to security, I looked at my new friend and told him, "I know you do not believe in God, but I can see Him in you even though you do not believe in Him. He loves you."

I looked into his eyes and the look on his face was one of – shock.

He was stunned and had tears slowly coming down his cheeks. I realized that of all the arguments I had used to prove the existence of God, it was not theological proofs that had moved him to experience a graced moment. It came with the mysterious force of love that hit him faster than his reason could grasp. Jesus spoke through me and that taste of a divine moment in time was a greater proof of the existence of God than any argument I could muster up during our conversation. It was a quiet "wow" moment for him. When I think of him, I claim his soul for Christ, and ask Jesus to have mercy on him and that my friend would not die without repenting.

This moment was a space of time where a Blessing came upon him. Somehow, some way, this gentleman realized and tasted a reality that moved him to tears. It spoke to him a Truth, a reality he could not yet understand – God loved him from all eternity even though he did not believe in God. We are priceless in the eyes of our Divine Parent even though we are not aware of the price that each of us has in God's heart – the Price of the Blood of His Co-Eternal Divine Son – Jesus.

My dear reader, please know that your worth to the Father is priceless. His blessing is upon you even if your father and mother did not or could not give you the Blessing.

4. Parents form a positive and empowering image of the future of their children.

When parents know their child by giving them the Blessing unconditionally, they really know their child. They notice the child's strengths and weaknesses. Being a father and mother must include a prayerfulness that seeks to discern and see reality, seeing their children through the eyes of God. This is wisdom. We might feel, "How can I see from God's perspective for I am only a human being and I am full of limitations?" We are told in the book of Proverbs,

> "Trust in the LORD with all your heart, on your own intelligence rely not; In all your ways be mindful of him, and he will make straight your paths. Be not wise in your own eyes, fear the LORD and turn away from evil..." (Prov 3:5-7)

We must be parents of integrity who seek the face of God and His insight on our children's paths as seen from an eternal perspective. He has a plan for them. We are told of Jeremiah when he was called to be a prophet,

> "Before I formed you in the womb I knew you, before you were born I dedicated you, a prophet to the nations I appointed you." (Jer 1:5)

So, we must seek God's insight first. Many parents form their children to be successful, to be "happy." What does it mean to be happy? Does it mean to have a lot of money? Many people do and are miserable. We were created for more than time and space, for more than anything or anyone can give us. I often meet families that brag that their "little Jimmy" is first in his class or captain of the football team and their daughter is the prom queen. They base the success of their parenting on their child's achievements. Yet this does not impress God. We are told in Matthew 19:30 that "many who are the first will be last and the last will be first."

God does see things very differently. One of my favorite passages of Scripture in Isaiah clearly states, "For my thoughts are not your thoughts, nor are your ways my ways – says the LORD." (Is. 55:8) So, we need a perspective of heaven to help our children figure out God's dream, His will from all eternity.

I know a woman who had almost died giving birth to her last two children. She was advised to have a tubal ligation. The doctors insisted she would die and leave her children orphaned if she were to become pregnant. She decided to have the tubal ligation. After the nurse had put the gas mask on her face to "put her under" she took off the gas mask. The doctor and nurses were shocked. The woman insisted, "I must not have the tubal ligation."

They argued with her, saying "You will die if you do not have this done and get pregnant." She was unmoved by their arguments. The doctor told her he would try to look more closely at her condition and see if through surgery he could help treat the condition that made her almost die twice. When she had awakened the doctor told her, "If before I believed you should not get pregnant, I realized your condition is more delicate than I first believed. You must not get pregnant!"

Four months later she did get pregnant – **and the book you have in your hands is written by one of the babies she conceived.** The other baby, my twin brother, is also a priest who also founded a religious community in Peru. Man's wisdom said, "You cannot get pregnant." God said, "I will then conceive two babies." His ways are not our ways. We must discover His way and will.

What is our part of the deal? We must pray and do our best to remain faithful. Avoid sin that is chosen intentionally. One thing is to sin out of weakness, but it is another thing is to plan it and choose it deliberately. In the book of Wisdom, we are told, "Because into a soul that plots evil wisdom enters not, nor dwells she in a body under debt of sin." (Wis 1:4) We need the perspective of heaven for our children.

A word on birth control and contraception: We must seek God's will in every area of our family life. This includes following the Church's teaching that every marital act should be open to life and that contraceptive methods are always to be avoided. Some couples, for serious reasons, choose to abstain from marital intimacy to avoid pregnancy at certain times, which the Church supports.

You might be thinking, "Come on Padre, you are priest and have no idea what it is like to have to abstain and be married." If you live out, for example, the Billings Method[9] of natural family

---

[9] The Billings Method of natural family planning has a 97 – 99% success rate, when used correctly with the intention of avoiding a pregnancy. Please note that the beauty of NFP methods is that they can be used to help achieve a pregnancy as well. NFP methods are never contraceptive in themselves--they do change the nature of the act--even if they can be misused for selfish ends (this is why prayer, communication, and discernment of the Lord's will are paramount for all couples). For more information about the Billings Method,

planning (NFP), which is in accord with Church teaching, you only must abstain between seven and ten days a month.[10]

I must abstain – not for seven to ten days a month, not for a month, not for a year, not for decade – but for my life. Believe me, this priest and all priests (and consecrated religious and single people) know what it means to abstain. I am a healthy man and a Latin. Yet it is God's will for me to be a celibate and to learn to receive and give love as a celibate in this time in history. I have been a priest for over three decades and I believe more in celibacy than when I was first ordained.

God's will has become the only point to the question of happiness. I am only unhappy when I have NOT done His will during the day. Now you, who are couples that that need to prepare your children to see God's will – you must also do so in every area of your life as a couple. God's will stretches you out at times right to your breaking point. You will not break; you will become more "you" by becoming God's. He alone knows the plans He has in mind for you. We are told in Jeremiah 29:11-13, "For I

---

please see the official website for this method at https://billings.life/en/.

[10] Of course, couples may discern the need to abstain for longer periods of time each month due to health or other circumstances

know well the plans I have in mind for you, says the LORD, plans for your welfare, not for woe! Plans to give you a future of hope. When you call me, when you go to pray to me, I will listen to you. When you look for me, you will find me. Yes, when you seek me with all your heart."

When parents have given their children the Blessing, they have invested their whole being to build the unconditional love of God into the lives of their children. There is a foundation that has been laid in the children's hearts. Sirach 3:9 says, "For a father's blessing gives firm roots..." It gives strong and generous hearts.

When one has received the Blessing, he lives life in order to give what was given. If one has not received the Blessing, one seeks to receive love more than to give the Blessing to someone else. Our Lord Himself said, "…It is more blessed to give than to receive." (Acts 20:35) Where do we find in Scriptures stories of parents who gave the Blessing and could then describe or prophesy positively their child's future? I will give some examples:

Isaac describes to his son Jacob this image after blessing him,

> "May God give to you of the dew of the heavens and of the fertility of the earth

abundance of grain and wine. Let peoples serve you, and nations pay your homage; Be master of your brothers, and may your mother's sons bow down to you. Cursed be those who curse you, and blessed be those who bless you." (Gen. 27:28-29).

Although Jacob received the Blessing in a "dishonorable" way, he heard his father describe the future of his being blessed. So also do we see Jacob describe to his son Judah his blessedness,

"You, Judah, shall your brothers praise – your hand on the neck of your enemies; the sons of your father shall bow down to you. Judah, like a lion's whelp, you have grown up on prey, my son. He crouches like a lion recumbent, the king of beasts – who would dare rouse him? The scepter shall never depart from Judah, or the mace from between his legs, while tribute is brought to him, and he receives the people's homage." (Gen 49:8-10)

So too does Jesus describe something of the blessedness of being one of His followers.

> "In my Father's house there are many dwelling places. If there were not, would I have told you that I am going to prepare a place for you? And if I go and prepare a place for you, I will come back again and take you to myself, so that where I am you also may be." (John 14:2-3)

Parents cannot truly know their children unless the parents live a life of prayer, and thus are able to see what gifts God has given their children and the plans He might have for them. The point I wish to emphasize is that a "positive" picture must be conveyed to a child. One might say, "I see God has given you these gifts. He might be calling you to be a doctor...an honest lawyer...a good priest or religious." The key point is to create a picture for your child that calls him/her to do God's will.

God has a "dream" of what St. Paul beautifully describes in 1 Corinthians 2:9, "But as it is written: What eye has not seen, and ear has not heard, and what has not entered the human heart, what God has prepared for those who love him." I did not receive the Blessing from my father or mother. (I will discuss this in more detail later.)

God, being well aware of this, placed a priest in my life who was my teacher of Scripture in the seminary. My last exam before ordination was an oral exam with this fine and holy priest. This priest did not know me other than as his student in various classes of Scripture. When I was done with the exam he told me, "You can put the Bible down. Remember what I am about to tell you. The day will come when I will hear about you and I will say, 'I knew him once...' He began to describe my future and "paint" an image of my future as a priest that came from no other than from my Heavenly Father. This priest described part of what I am now doing. I received this part of the Father's Blessing through him.

This priest might have noticed my father wound. Yet God, my Eternal Parent, knew my need for words that would help me to "fly" and one day begin a community whose charism is to heal the family, though I myself came from a family which lacked so much. The priest's inspired words on that day have often come to mind when things are difficult, and they propel me forward to persevere through thick and thin.

That is what the Blessing does. It gives us a confidence for God to fulfill His dream in us as St. Paul tells us, "I am confident of this, that the one who began a good work in you will continue to complete it until the day of Christ Jesus." (Phil. 1:6) Because I have known the Blessing I trust in the power of God. I realize all is gift because the Blessing is a gift. We could never earn it. And now we come to what is the fifth aspect of the Blessing: Parental correction.

5. Parental correction and discipline springs from love.

When a child has not received the Blessing, he sees any rule or correction not as an act of love but as tyrannical. Dr. David Stoop, a Christian therapist, in his book *Making Peace with Your Father* calls the father the "the lawgiver," and states that this aspect of fatherhood is of primary importance between the ages of six and twelve. He writes, "Lawgiving is a role unique to fathers. This does not mean that mothers do not train children to distinguish right from wrong or that they do not provide any family discipline…If I know Dad is there and that he is involved in my life, I will have an inner sense of security and structure that goes beyond the concept of laws or of knowing right from wrong." [11]

This last point, parental correction, is taken from the book of Hebrews. It is at first hidden, painful and we dislike it due to our fallen nature. We hate to be disciplined and corrected. Because of pride, we have a slant, a tendency that wars against God – in other words, concupiscence. I believe that part of our fallen nature that resents that we

---

[11] Stoop, Ph.D., David. *Making Peace with the Father*. Page 60.

are not #1 – that we are not God. St. Paul spoke of this inner battle in us:

> "What I do, I do not understand. For I do not do what I want, but I do what I hate. Now if I do what I do not want, I concur that the law is good. So now it is no longer I who do it, but sin that dwells in me. For I know that good does not dwell in me, that is, in my flesh. The willing is ready at hand, but doing the good is not. For I do not do the good I want, but I do the evil I do not want. Now if (I) do what I do not want, it is no longer I who do it, but sin that dwells in me. So, then, I discover the principle that when I want to do right, evil is at hand." (Rom 7:15-21)

We all struggle with this. We resent it when things do not go our way. When our will is not allowed to be done. We say we want God's will, but that is far easier said than done. Let me give you some examples of what I mean using Scripture:

God asks for generosity when dealing with the poor. St. Mother Teresa of Calcutta used to teach that we ought to give until it hurts. In the book of Tobit we are told,

> "Give alms from your possessions. Do not turn your face away from any of the poor, and God's face will not be turned away from you. Son, give alms in proportion to what you own. If you have great wealth, give alms out of your abundance; if you have but little, distribute even some of that. But do not hesitate to give alms; ... Alms are a worthy offering in the sight of the Most High for all who give them." (Tob 4:7-8, 11)

Yet we Catholics, of all the Christian Churches, are known to give the least. We are told in chapter 12 of this same book that alms giving, "saves one from death and expiates every sin." (Tob 12:9).

What we have is not our own. We are stewards or administrators of God's gifts. We must use what we need and dedicate the rest for use in helping others achieve God's Kingdom. I used to know a millionaire who told me in confidence that he lived by the 10% rule. I asked him if he tithed. He answered me, "I am getting old. I have lived too well. I stay with 10% of what I make and give away 90% to God's work." If we have been blessed with financial gain, we are expected to be generous.

A woman in Peru who is very wealthy and married to a member of one of the wealthiest families in Peru asked to speak to me. She asked me, "How is a wealthy person saved?" I told her that a wealthy person is saved in the same way as a poor person, by Christ dying for our sins. This is a free gift. It is a free gift, but it is not a cheap gift. It costs and asks of us a TOTAL giving of our lives to love God with our whole existence.

This demands a response of losing our whole life to find it by doing His will on earth, for "whoever wishes to save his life will lose it, but whoever loses his life for my sake and that of the gospel will save it. What profit is there for one to gain the whole world and forfeit his life? What could one give in exchange for his life?" (Mark 8:35-37). How many are willing to give up their plans for God's will? In Matthew 7:21 it is written "Not everyone who says to me, 'Lord, Lord,' will enter the kingdom of heaven, but only the one who does the will of my Father in heaven." What could be worth more than the salvation of our souls?

Let me give one more example, the question of living together before marriage. In the United States, multiple studies show that couples who live together prior to marriage are more likely to end up divorcing than couples who do not live together before marriage. In any case, to live together outside of marriage (presuming sexual relations) is to fornicate. St. Paul tells us to flee fornication. Jesus tells us,

> "You have heard that it was said, 'You shall not commit adultery.' But I say to you, everyone who looks at a woman with lust has already committed adultery with her in his heart." (Matt 5:27-28)

When I lived in the United States as a young priest, I would say 90% of the couples that came to me to celebrate their wedding were living together. We do not like doing God's will and we have a silent, but very real, declaration of war against Him. St. Paul was right. We will discuss why this might be the case, and how this innate bent against God's will might be related to not receiving the Blessing.

What is a parent to do when a child refuses to obey? The child must be disciplined for his/her own sake. God does no less. We read in the book of Hebrews,

> "My son, do not disdain the discipline of the Lord or lose heart when reproved by him; for whom the Lord loves, he disciplines; he scourges every son he acknowledges. Endure your trials as discipline; God treats you as sons. For what 'son' is there whom his father does not discipline? If you are without discipline, in which all have shared, you are

> not sons but bastards. Besides this, we have had our earthly fathers discipline us, and we respected them. Should we not [then] submit all the more to the Father of spirits and live? They disciplined us for a short time as seemed right to them, but he does so for our benefit, in order that we may share his holiness. At the time, all discipline seems a cause not for joy but for pain, yet later it brings the peaceful fruit of righteousness to those who are trained by it." (Heb 12:6-11)

Although the focus is on God's Paternal correction, here are a few words on parental correction and how this correction can bond parent and child, and turn out to be a deep experience of the Blessing.

I have a dear friend from my first parish whom I saw one Monday morning sitting in the back of the Church speaking with his eldest son, who was very young at the time. I sat there hearing him teach his son. The boy had not behaved well at the previous Sunday Mass. The father was explaining to him what goes on at Mass and why we must really try to be open to all that God wishes to give us. The young boy sat on his father's lap, listening to his father speak lovingly but firmly. My friend never took his eyes off his son. The son, though corrected, was held in his father's arms. I sat there and thought, "Is this not what

God does with us when He corrects us?" I asked my friend recently over lunch if he remembers that conversation with his son. He answered he did.

I once had to correct a brother of ours who broke a window in our house. He had arrived by car at our house after Mass, and on my arrival, he came to me and said, "Father, I should have waited. I just broke a window trying to get into the house. I should have waited. It was my fault. I am sorry." I was angry and must sadly admit that I have often lost my temper over trivial things, and have had to ask forgiveness from my community. But here God caught me before I reacted in an angry manner. I thought, "He admitted he was wrong. He admitted what he did was stupid and asked forgiveness." What else could he do?

I sensed it was me that also had to learn something. I opened my arms to him and received him. It was a blessed moment. A moment of correction became a moment of bonding, where our hearts truly touched. It didn't separate us, it bonded us.

In the past years I have realized and learned that moments of correction can become moments to pass on the Blessing. Such moments have become opportunities to bond. First one must listen and listen deeply – to pray for God's insight so somehow a difficult moment can become a graced moment – where grace is seen at work and we end up even thanking God for the difficult moment. At times I have even ended up crying with the brother or sister involved during a moment of correction, and then we both end up laughing in each other's arms.

I have realized after many years that anger has never served me well. I was born with a quick temper. In Spanish we say, "This person is like a match that is lit." That described my angry reactions. The founding of the community was first meant to convert me. How often I realized my need to say, "Mea culpa." I grew up in a family where just one feeling was allowed to be expressed, and that was anger. I used to cry out to God to deliver me from my angry reactions. I KNEW that Proverbs states that the "just man falls seven times a day." I realized every time I got angry I over-corrected. It was not a graced moment.

Before I could get past my all too easy inclination to anger, I first had to experience how bad this sin of anger tasted. St. Paul, when speaking about anger, tells us in his letter to the Ephesians, "Be angry but do not sin; do not let the sun set on your anger, and do not leave room for the devil." (Eph 4:26-27). I slowly began to see that my anger blinded me. It filled me with what St. Ignatius of Loyola called distorted thinking. These distorted thoughts are diabolical and a lie! I used to think that if I felt strongly about something that my perspective was correct.

However, I later realized that too often I found myself having to ask forgiveness for my unkind words or over-reacting due to my angry feelings.

Then I was given a CD with a wonderful talk by a Canadian deacon psychologist named Deacon Bob McDonald on <u>Anger and Forgiveness</u>.[12] My intention here is not to summarize this wonderful talk or give lengthy reflection on overcoming anger. This CD was sent from heaven. In it, the wonderful Deacon states that *anger should never be the moment to choose to respond.* We ought to disconnect for a moment or however long it takes – whether it be the length of time it takes to pray a decade of the rosary or 15 minutes of praise and even singing to Jesus. I began to see how differently I saw things, once I disconnected from my angry and distorted thinking.

Now when I feel anger, I tell myself "You are blind. You cannot trust your perspective at this moment. You will feel differently about this later." I tell you that I never regret not responding to a moment of anger. My purpose in discussing anger is not to give a full teaching on it, but only to state for the purpose of this book that, as my anger has been put into check, I refuse to respond in anger to a person during a moment of discipline or correction, making the encounter into truly an experience of the Blessing.

---

[12] This CD also is available in video format on https://formed.org/.

David Stoop, Ph.D., author of *Making Peace with Your Father*, wrote that when there is nurturing by the father, "a father helps his children learn to make decisions about right from wrong for themselves. It is not just a matter of 'following orders.' When it comes to rules and standards of behavior, children operate on a 'show me,' not on a 'tell me' basis. Children need to see morality modeled, struggled with, confronted and dealt with realistically and honestly. A father who is comfortably balanced in his lawgiving role is able to demonstrate his sense of integrity and morality by the way he relates to his children, not just proclaim it to them." [13] *Such moments of correction can become an opportunity for deeper bonding between father and child.*

My dear reader, I do not know what you experienced in your childhood during moments of correction. If you are like me, such moments were very painful. I have had to unlearn much to make room for God's instruction, as He used exactly the unpleasant moment to open my eyes. What I dislike was exactly what God was using to teach me.

Moments of conflict have become moments of greatest Blessing. Where before I was blinded by my initial feelings of anger, now I must humbly admit in truth that

---

[13] Stoop, D. *Making Peace with Your Father*. Pages 60-61.

the angry feelings blinded me. I thank our Lord for His infinite patience and light to show me how wrong I was, though I thought I saw clearly at the time. Anger is a human emotion. With St. Paul I asked and discovered, "... Who will deliver me from this mortal body? Thanks be to God through Jesus Christ our Lord. Therefore, I myself, with my mind, serve the law of God but, with my flesh, the law of sin." (Rom 7:24-25)

What grace from my Eternal Parent, my Father! He so loved me as a son that He corrected me, because He was treating as me as His son. Praise God for His mercy!!

Chapter Two – My Own Childhood Experience, the Absence of the Blessing: The Father Wound

I did not learn to cry, really cry, until I was twenty years old. I come from a family of seven children. When I faced the truth that what to me seemed "normal" in my upbringing was in fact not normal, I also was able to work through the absence of the Blessing from my father and mother. Since then, all has become gift. I choose to share my own experience of the absence of the Blessing. Why? To give you hope. If you have not known the Blessing, like I did not, you can heal and learn from even very painful past events.

I pray that as you read my own experience, you too will allow yourself to be led by the Holy Spirit to those parts of your life that were not parented lovingly. There is hope from our Eternal Parent, God the Father. Psalm 27:10

(RSV) states, "Even if my father and mother forsake me, the LORD will take me in." To not receive the Blessing means experiencing a real sense of abandonment on some level. However, most parents have done their best to bring up their children and love them the best they could.

I believe this about my own parents. My father's name was Frank Kingsbury Scott and my mother's name was Rosa Maria Scott Chavanches. I grew up with parents who loved each other deeply, and who were affectionate with each other. For my father, my mother was his "queen." Rarely do I remember them arguing with one other. Daily my parents taught me about the love between a husband and a wife, as I witnessed the love they showed to each other. They were in so many ways an example, to me and my siblings, in living the vocation of marriage.

My father was a very just and honest man. Having been an orphan himself, my father had a special place in his life and heart for those in need. When I would complain about the food at the dinner table, he would tell me, "You have never had to be hungry. Eat your food." I did.

And my father was no wimp. He had boxed as a young man, and photographs of him from that time show a person who looked like Tarzan. Yet he never worked through his anger and hurt of his upbringing with an alcoholic father. As a young boy he entered his house one day and saw his father dead drunk as he lay on the floor. My father never healed on this side of eternity from that wound called the "father-wound."

I once asked my father, "Tell me about Papapa (my grandfather)." His answer to me was a short and gruff "It is none of your business." That is as much as I was able to get out of my father about his childhood. My father never dealt in a healthy way with his pain other than trying to be strong and not discussing his pain at all.

So, what do you think happened? You probably guessed easily and correctly that my father expressed his pain and anger in the wrong way. He was violent (though not with my mother). I was one of his main targets – receiving blows to my face and body. Once I was so savagely beaten that my second oldest brother thought I had gotten in a fight with five young men. And father was also not one to talk much or share his feelings. I never really got to know him and he never really got to know me. Yes, we kissed him on the cheek upon his arrival home from work. Yet never did my father tell me he loved me, though I know he did.

In many ways my house never felt like home. If my father came home in a bad mood, it was time to avoid being home like one avoids the plague. Instead, I would escape, going somewhere, anywhere, with my friends. These escapes became my "bunker," my place of protection and safety that kept me clear of the "artillery fire" that came from my father's episodes of anger. Our dinner times were times when children were seen but not heard. If he was in a bad mood and I wanted to share something about my day, I would hear from his end of the table his voice shouting, "Quiet!" And that was the end of the conversation.

On my seventh birthday, my father had a heart attack which almost made us orphans. From then on, my mother lived with a great fear of losing my dad and her becoming a young widow. (When my mother was young, she lost her father in a tragic hit and run car accident.) Mother was fearful of having my father die of a heart attack while becoming angry, so when he exploded, she would raise her finger over her lips for us children to immediately behave and not make another sound. My mother's goal was to keep my father at peace at all costs. This was her daily "mission." All else was secondary.

When I played on a sports team, my parents never came to see me play. If my team won the championship, I would attend the award ceremony alone. At the ceremony, I sat at a table alone waiting for my name to be called and I would walk up to receive my trophy with no applause. The other families must have wondered, "Where are his parents?"

Planning to come and see me play in a sporting event was nowhere on my parents' radar screen. It was never even discussed as a possibility. For me, the absence of my parents was just normal and usual. If anyone would have asked me then, "Does it is bother you that your parents are not at your baseball, football games, and tennis tournaments?" I probably would have looked at them with an expression that could not understand why such a question even crossed their minds. I only knew and lived my reality, and I acted as if all was fine and well. The important thing was that my team won the championship, and I got a trophy.

I have a memory of being about 14 years old and training hard as a tennis player, because my dream was to play tennis professionally. My father was walking our dog across the park near the tennis courts, and I noticed him stop and watch me play for about a minute. I suddenly began trying to hit some incredible shots to impress my father who was watching me. This was my one chance for him to notice me. Again, as when playing in other team events, my teammates would have their family members cheering them on. And once again, it was normal never to have my parents there.

During my elementary school years, when we had school family picnics, all families were invited and all my friends had their parents and brothers and sisters with them enjoying their dinner on the school grounds. My twin and I would walk around visiting various friends and their families. We went from family to family and sat with them. We never felt unusual or not normal that all the children had their parents and family members with them and we did not. At the time, this all seemed not to affect me. We had never known things to be any other way for us.

Let us return to my mother, Rosa. She too never dealt well with her pain. She was an enabler and developed her skills of denial to perfection. She never thought my father needed to look at his past and the cause of his anger and pain. She would just say, "Poor dad. He is just that way."

The result of living with the absence of a close relationship with either my father or mother left a crater-sized hole in my heart which, in my middle teenage years, led me to try to fill that emptiness with a hedonistic lifestyle of sin. Not that I blame my parents for my sinful lifestyle. I do not.

There is no need to get into details but just know I have been forgiven very much. In fact, if the police had been present and caught me in the act of my sinful choices, I would have been arrested. God is merciful – very merciful! Still, during this time in my life I resented my father and hated him.

At the youthful age of twenty, after having had the worst vacation in Peru as I visited a girlfriend of mine, I returned very disgusted with life. It was a few months later that I had my encounter with Jesus in my bedroom. I would have never thought I was "searching for God." I had many friends; my career as a commercial artist was getting off the ground. I had a car and a girlfriend. All *seemed* well.

Yet inside my heart, I was empty and lonely. A friend of mine wrote in my High School yearbook, "Philip, I have never seen anybody party like you. Just don't get caught." That gives you an idea of the state of my soul – a life that was anything but chaste.

Chapter Three – "Get two handkerchiefs..."

One Saturday evening I found myself at home. Sin had begun to taste bad, which was a great gift from the Holy Spirit though I did not realize this yet. I did not know I was searching for God and that my way of life was a reaction to my father and mother wounds. I knelt down at the end of my bed and told Jesus, "I do not even know You, but I give You my life."

Next evening, I picked up a cable TV guide to watch a movie with porn. I heard a voice in me that said, "If you have decided to follow Me, you must stop this." My heart and my faith told me it was the voice of Jesus. His voice spoke with love but in a firm way. I put the guide down.

For the next three or four nights I was awakened at 12:30 a.m. by a very loving, merciful, powerful Presence in my bedroom. Without choosing to discuss the topic of my sinfulness, I could not stop crying about my sinful lifestyle. I experienced a "look of love and mercy" that is hard to describe. And although I could not see Jesus, I knew He was in my bedroom each time I woke up. He "loved" my sinful lifestyle out of me. I cried and cried during each "visitation" of my merciful Savior. He did not condemn me. I would say I experienced what Pentecostals and Charismatics call the "Baptism of the Holy Spirit." [14] On each successive night that this visitation occurred, the same experience as the first night's visitation would begin once more.

I believe my initial encounter was so powerful because of the lack of an emotional connection with my parents and family. I asked my mother for a Bible and I began to devour Sacred Scripture. Literally, Jesus had freed me from a lifestyle of mortal sin – overnight (see 1 Jn.5:16). I went to the people I had hurt and asked for their forgiveness. To girls I had used sexually, I also asked forgiveness, and even sent cassettes asking for forgiveness to one girl who was overseas.

---

[14] From Catholic Answers website – "This expression 'baptism in the Holy Spirit' is used in the charismatic renewal to refer to an experience of an intensified awareness of the presence and power of the Holy Spirit…Even so, the use of the word *baptism* can lead to a misunderstanding, since this experience is not a sacrament instituted by Christ but rather a new awareness of the life given to Christians in the sacraments of baptism and confirmation." [All Christians are called to life in the Holy Spirit, and to exercise the gifts and charisms given to them.]

They all thought (including my family and twin brother) that I had gone crazy. I began to give things away to the poor. Life changed very quickly, though I found little support at home.

I cannot get into every detail of my initial conversion experience, but eventually the girl I dated in Latin America broke up with me. She could not handle my overnight conversion experience – I scared the poor girl to death. I went from being a hedonistic boyfriend to a "Bible-thumping" boyfriend who wanted everyone to meet Jesus – and meet Him RIGHT NOW! My hunger for Christ and the Scriptures grew and kept growing.

Yet I became a Catholic-on-fire who did not know his Catholic faith well. My brother-in-law who had become a Baptist-Charismatic (an interesting combination) noticed that my life had radically changed. He began to "fellowship" with me and introduced me to faithful Christians of different churches. At first these new Christian friends were incredibly supportive and loving until the question of my Catholic faith would come up. They challenged me with questions on Mary, Purgatory, confession to a priest, the Papacy and other matters. I had no answers to give them or to give to myself.

I began to believe the Church had lied to me. The Church had tricked me, so eventually I hung around more with my non-Catholic Christian friends and my anti-Catholic brother-in-law. I no longer saw myself as a Catholic but as a "born-again Christian." I went to Wednesday-night church services with my brother-in-law. My father told me after hearing me argue with my aunt who was a staunch Catholic, "If you live under my roof you must go to Mass."

Without knowing it, my father was serving as God's instrument. I no longer believed in many of the Church's teachings, and no longer called myself a Catholic; I could not afford to leave home; and I was dearly trying to convert my twin brother to Christ – and showing him that remaining in the Catholic Church meant he was not a Christian. I was pegged a "fanatic."

As time passed and I became more of an anti-Catholic, I met a wonderful and beautiful girl. There was one problem – she was a Catholic. She went to a Spanish Mass in my home parish. In that parish church, I felt like a fish out of water. Since I wanted to ask this girl out, I decided to attend that Spanish Mass and, after the final blessing, ask her out on a date. She accepted my invitation.

But our Lord had other reasons for drawing me to this Mass besides my wanting to ask this young lady out. To my surprise, there was a priest who was a biblical scholar from Spain who presided at the Mass. He was on fire and yet had a beautiful gentleness about him. He connected very well with young adults who were searching for meaning in their lives.

I was awestruck as he preached. It did not make sense, I thought to myself, "Catholics do not use the Bible." This priest did. In fact, I learned that if a person attended Mass for three years, he will go through the Church's three cycles of Mass readings – in other words, he would have virtually completed the entire Bible. And if attentive to the Mass readings during the liturgy of the Word, one would hear the Bible read from Genesis to the Book of Revelation.

After all, according to Romans 10:17, "Thus faith comes from what is heard, and what is heard comes through the word of Christ." To my surprise, this priest quoted from the Bible he held in his hand and explained the Word in a way that made the Scriptures come alive, and enabled us to apply Scriptures to our daily lives. I sat on the edge of my pew, blown away!

My purpose in writing this book is not to give you a full account of the biblical and historical reasons why I am a Catholic (and a convinced one I am) and priest. I briefly share my conversion story with you to point out that my main issue with the Catholic Church was not the papacy, Mary and other teachings of our Catholic Faith, which are so often questioned by other fellow Christians who often misunderstand us (the Catholic Church).

In reality, my issues with the Catholic faith sprung from and were rooted in my unresolved relationship with my father. Though it was important for me to discover the biblical and historical evidence for being Catholic, as well as the Apostolic and other Fathers of the Church, the issue was more an issue of the heart, a deep wound now often called the "father-wound." Later I will discuss how the Father, my Eternal Parent, healed the absence of the Blessing that should be given by our parents.

But for now, let us return to my account of how God led my heart and head back to the Church – back to the Mass that I attended initially for the main reason of asking the young lady out. After accepting my invitation to a date, she introduced me to this priest who was so dynamic and so very biblically grounded. He invited us to a Catholic gathering at The Catholic University in Washington D.C. This gathering of other young professionals and young adults was part of what I know to be the movement called Communion and Liberation.[15]

---

[15] From the movement's website, https://english.clonline.org/cl, comes this – "Born in Milan in the 1950s, today the Movement has spread to ninety countries. Communion and Liberation, in its essence, is a proposal for education in the Catholic faith. It is an education that doesn't end at a certain age, but lasts a lifetime because it is always being renewed and deepened."

The gathering was led by three biblical scholars who were priests, and two additional scholars who were religious sisters. My date and I went every Sunday evening and I found myself slowly falling in love with my Catholic faith and the Church. I heard and learned the biblical and historical basis for being Catholic. The early Church was without doubt Catholic, and the Holy Sacrifice of the Mass was their form of worship.

I had truly found my home was in Rome.

My girlfriend and I had a relationship that became stronger and closer. From the beginning of my relationship, I was interiorly guided to a chaste life. I told her, "We cannot even French kiss," and I explained that I was called to protect her purity. If we kissed that way, I said, it could lead to other forms of foreplay. She accepted this, and I began learning and practicing the virtue that a Christian man is meant to be a protector of purity.

We men are called to protect our purity and the purity of the women in our lives. This need to *protect* is at the core of our masculinity. It is in our nature as men. Deep inside we want to be "heroic" in doing the right thing, God's will. We like challenges. Our relationship deepened and eventually I asked my girlfriend for her hand in marriage. She accepted.

Here we were: We were deeply Catholic; wanted to serve God as a Catholic couple; and wanted to glorify God by the way we lived out relationship. We had a beautiful Christ-centered relationship. What else could God want? We were planning our honeymoon, and the priesthood certainly was nowhere on my radar screen. Before we made the engaged encounter weekend, I told her, "Why not go on another retreat with our Sunday evening group." She loved the idea. So, we were off for one weekend to the mountains of Virginia. It was very romantic and I remember it had snowed.

On this romantic retreat we looked like the "couple" of the group. Everything seemed so perfect. When Saturday night arrived, I sat holding her hand as we listened to a talk on being a "fisher" of men. At some point in the talk, I was enveloped by a mysterious silence. I was no longer aware of anyone in the room but Father Javier, Jesus and me.

I heard these words in my soul, "My son, leave everything and come follow me."

I was stunned. I asked, "Everything?" "Even my fiancé?" The answer came, "Everything." The reality of this call to the priesthood filled my whole being. Again, to say the least – I was stunned. My girlfriend noticed that the rest of the weekend I was incredibly quiet. She asked me, "Is something wrong?" I told her everything was "fine."

As the weeks passed, she still noticed my pre-occupation with something. I was not willing to share what that something was. Instead, I was hoping my experience was just some Peruvian or Hispanic fervor – that I was going through a phase that would soon go away like a bad cold. It did not. My fiancé would try to get me to talk about what was really on my mind. I had to tell her. I broke down and cried. She and I had been happy, chaste and even wanting to serve God and truly seek holiness as a Catholic couple and eventually as a Catholic family. I usually do not do things "half-way." We were not planning on being a Catholic family that was mediocre. I thought God was satisfied with my relationship.

But did Jesus want anything more? Yes. He wanted me, and only for Him. It was very painful to see my fiancé cry, and I knew well that my call to be a priest was the cause. I did not want to make her suffer. Yet I knew I could not get married for she deserved someone wanting to be a good husband – and I wanted to be a good priest. This was one of the most difficult and painful moments of my life. Yet I believe I am now living who I was created to be from all eternity. Jeremiah 29:11 tells us, "For I know the plans I have in mind for you…"

God alone knew what His dream was for me. *When your father's and mother's blessing are missing from your life, you try to do all things and solve all things by yourself.* "It is up to me" often is the gut response. I couldn't go to my parents to be vulnerable with them. I could not even go to my twin, as he did not understand either. I felt very alone, misunderstood and isolated.

One might have a growing ugly gnawing feeling that he did not receive the Blessing. God is unlike a human medical doctor, who during surgery closes the wound with stitches. God the Divine Healer *opens* and exposes the wound, which HURTS. There is a purpose – a divine purpose. God allows suffering because it is necessary to open our lives to the only One who can "make all things better." Suffering – going through the process from "pain to peace" is healing, as it is transformative to take you from the unblessedness of whatever wounded home life you have lived to the Blessedness of life in the Eternal Family, the Trinity. This is meant to begin not only in heaven but here on earth.

Please believe me! Behind the "big bad wolf" of suffering is not death, but rather an invitation to experience your adoption, by baptism, as a son or daughter of the Father. God has been calling you and me – from the depths of our pain. He calls each of us to live as "sons" and "daughters" in the Son, who alone is eternally Son, and He is Jesus.

So how does God, our eternal Parent, see our pain, tears of our upbringing and missing the Blessing? In 1985, I was in my first year of theology at Mount St. Mary's Seminary in Emmitsburg, Maryland. We seminarians were having a day of prayer. For a day of prayer, a priest was invited to preach, and we spent the day in prayer before our Eucharistic Lord and Divine Healer, Jesus. As I was entering the chapel, I sensed this invitation in my heart, "My son, bring two handkerchiefs."

I got two handkerchiefs and sat in the first row of pews. I had a sense Jesus wanted to go deeper into my wounded heart. He wanted to show me a perspective of my Eternal Parent that I had not seen before. (There are things that must be shown to us. They must be revealed.) When the priest exposed the Blessed Sacrament, I looked at Jesus and I told Him, "Jesus, I am not afraid to cry in front of my brothers in the seminary. Why have you asked me to bring two handkerchiefs? Is not one enough? Let us not make a scene."

Often in my life I had made a silent scream, and at other times a scream that was not silent, because of having been put in a home where there was little love expressed by parents to children. Yet at the beginning of this day of prayer, I had a silence in my heart inviting me to expect something that reminds me of St. Paul's words in his first letter to the Corinthians,

> "…eye has not seen, and ear has not heard, and what has not entered the human heart, what God has prepared for those who love him." (1Cor 2:9)

God wants us to look up into His eyes that are filled with pain, a pain that heals. This desire comes from the Father's Eternal Heart that has longed to share His Parental pain when He sees one of His sons or daughters suffer.

When the priest giving the day of prayer finished preaching, again I asked Our Lord, "Why two handkerchiefs?" The answer came as a voice – without a voice. It filled me, all of me. Then the answer came. I could never have guessed it in a million years. "One is for you and one is for Me." I went forward into the pew and cried.

The Lord showed me the Father's perspective of my being beaten. I was shown one memory after another of my father beating me, with me trying to stop the blows to my face and my father then kneeing me in my legs. I tried to block his blows with my hands, then I would feel a blow to my face. I cannot remember how long this lasted. Then

I saw Jesus next to my father and I could hear Jesus crying out with indignation, "Stop Frank!" Jesus was inconsolable and took this beating so very personally. Jesus cried in desperation to have my father stop, and Jesus' loving indignation filled me with a divine perspective.

The Father does not sit back and look at our pain coldly or with any detachment, or with an attitude of "offer it up" and "take it like a man." There was in Jesus a holy indignation. I do not remember how I got out of the chapel. I remember trying to walk and barely able to slide my feet forward, crying so hard I could not see where I was going. Just seeing Jesus react that way lifted me up to look into the face of my eternal Parent, my Father.

The impact of why that additional handkerchief was requested went through me like a torch – a Divine Flame of Love that touched every part of me. The impact was stronger than the blows of the many beatings I had experienced from my father. The truth of these painful memories was small and nearly eclipsed when compared to the truth of how heaven saw my pain. Eventually God's truth, His Eternal cry, the "Stop, Frank!" I heard was louder and more real than those dark memories.

The suffering was not the ultimate reality. What I saw and experienced with the two handkerchiefs in that chapel had become REALITY! The present filled with the Real Presence and was more real than the past filled with pain.

When I recall the memory now, there is peace. This is the Peace that Jesus promised in John 14:27,

> "Peace I leave with you; my peace I give to you. Not as the world gives do I give it to you. Do not let your hearts be troubled or afraid."

The world offers peace without pain. Jesus, however, allows suffering to show us to what point He is with us, to what point He understands us and to what point He has heard our cry. This is what I discovered. This was the beginning of my new understanding of how heaven views suffering.

I will stress the fact that my purpose for sharing some of my painful memories with my father is not to diminish the positive qualities in him. I wanted to give examples of what might cause a "father wound" and how Heaven (God) wishes to heal us. In fact, as I will later share, I believe God allowed this to prepare me to identify with so many families that live a family life with little love. My father and mother really did the best they could to parent us. So, I can tell you honestly there are no hard feelings or harbored resentments. All has become "gift."

In the next chapter, we will look at the role of the father in the emotional formation of his children. Then we will see what happens when a child does not receive the Blessing, as well as what happens when a child has received the Blessing.

Chapter Four – An Un-Parented Child turned Father Fathers with Many Difficulties

A father impacts the emotional development of his sons and daughters. There is a battle, a conflict within the heart of a child, adolescent or adult who has not been loved unconditionally – in other words, when he or she has not received the Blessing. I would like to briefly look at the role the father has in the formation of his sons and daughters. We will use the excellent book by David Stoop, Ph.D., *Making Peace with Your Father*.

The father as nurturer: "This role is of primary importance from birth to age five.

The children feel secure – valued because by being receptive to their children's emotions, nurturers validate the core of their children's identities. As the same time, nurturers model for their children the ability to take another other person's perspective." [16] What happens when a father cannot go beyond the nurturing role? Dr. Stoop states, the father "is incapable of setting clear limits for his children. When they do wrong, he is eager to understand. He is usually unwilling to confront them when they transgress his limits …" [17]

The father as lawgiver: "To be a balanced father, however, a man must be able to access and utilize the other roles as well as his primary role. The weakness of the nurturing father will be an inability to set firm limits for his children and follow through in enforcing them. Typically, the nurturing father needs to work especially hard at developing the law-giving role." [18] He needs to develop his role as the main disciplinarian. Here the heart (our nurturing) needs to be led by the head (our lawgiving). One needs to develop what the Church has called the discernment of spirits. The late Fr. John Hardon S.J., in his book *Pocket Catholic Dictionary,* described this process as: "The ability to distinguish whether a given idea or impulse in the soul comes from the good spirit or from the evil spirit. It may be an act of the virtue of prudence, or a special gift of supernatural grace, or both. In persons who are seriously intent on doing God's will, the good spirit is recognized by the peace of mind and

---

[16] Stoop, D. Making Peace with Your Father. Page 52.
[17] Pages 53-54. Ibid.
[18] Page 55, Ibid.

readiness for sacrifice that a given thought or desire produces in the soul. The evil spirit produces disturbance of mind and a tendency to self-indulgence." [19]

The word discern comes from the Latin *discernere*, which means to distinguish whether a particular idea or movement in the soul comes from God (or a good spirit, angel) or an evil spirit (a bad spirit). When some interior movement in the soul causes the soul to become inflamed with love of its Creator and Lord, if it causes the soul to shed tears that move to love of its Lord, either out of sorrow for one's sins, or for the Passion of Christ Our Lord, or because of other things directly connected with His service and praise – St. Ignatius calls this interior movement a spiritual consolation.

These spiritual consolations are reliably ascribed to God, as they lead to an increase of faith, hope and charity, and to an interior joy which calls and attracts to heavenly things, quieting the soul and giving it peace in its Creator.

However, movements can be ascribed to evil spirits such as those in persons who go from mortal sin to mortal sin, with the Enemy commonly proposing to these persons apparent pleasures, making them imagine sensual delights and pleasures in order to hold them more and make them grow in their vices and sins. St. Ignatius names these

---

[19] Hardon, S.J., J. *Pocket Catholic Dictionary*. Page 111.

interior movements contrary to spiritual consolations as spiritual desolations.

Desolations are movements such as darkness of soul, disturbance in it, movement to things low and earthly, the unquiet of different agitations and temptations, moving to lack of confidence, without hope or without love, and finally finding oneself lazy, tepid, sad, and as if separated from his Creator and Lord.[20]

St. Ignatius of Loyola taught that at such moments one must not make a decision. One should not decide on a particular course of action in moments of spiritual desolation for the movement can be trusted as coming from an evil spirit, the "father of lies." Why is this important? We often react and correct or discipline someone in a moment of anger, impatience or desolation. We do not see correctly. The correction might be necessary – just not at that particular moment.

A good question to ask ourselves is: What generally moves me to exercise my role as lawgiver or disciplinarian? Are we led by a sense of hopefulness, peace, a moment to instruct, a sense of quiet strength that comes from an impulse of the Holy Spirit? If this is the

---

[20] St. Ignatius' understanding of spiritual desolation, insofar as the causes or reasons, can involve our own sinfulness and/or a mysterious allowance by God for us to grow.

case, we are being led by the Spirit of God and we are acting as sons and daughters of God.

I would recommend asking Our Lord to send angels to the room to assist us in our discipline to make it an experience of love through instruction by God. When we are led by God, there is a sense of hopefulness, a quiet sense of "rightness." Even if the moment begins in a difficult way, God will give the words and the way to guide us in this "moment" of discipline. Often, we do not feel God's closeness during such moments but we must trust we are not alone – that He is parenting through us.

It is not just "me" or "I" acting within myself. Rather, it is "us," God AND me!

If we are led in this role as lawgiver with a sense of frustration, helplessness, fear, anger or the like, then we must see that it is not God leading to discipline, but that we are being led by an impulse to act coming from the Enemy. This process of learning to be led by the impulse of God is learned slowly and we can be sure that God wants us to learn this – and that He will allow ample opportunities to develop this sensitivity to the impulses of God and from God. It might be helpful if we review this process of being led by God step by step:

1. We need a good head-to-heart connection. I ask myself "What am I feeling?" Is it peace, joy, hopefulness, a sense of well-being? Or is it frustration, anger, discouragement, fear, a sense of hopelessness? What thoughts am I thinking? Would Jesus think these thoughts?

2. When a particular movement within me happens and moves me to act or say something, am I moved by love, a sense to be more generous, kindness, hopefulness, confidence? A sense of "rightness?" Is it in line with Scripture and official Church teaching (especially as expressed in the Catechism of the Catholic Church)? [21] If so, then I can trust this movement and that it is a moment that is given by God, brought about by God. He is about to do a work that is meant to open us up to His guidance, even in a moment of discipline.

3. But what if what moved me to act was a feeling of frustration, impatience, anger, fear, etc.? Then I must humbly admit that God did

---

[21] For more information on this subject, you are recommended to read *In School of the Holy Spirit*, by Father Jacques Phillipe. Full reference in the bibliography at the end of this book.

not lead me. Such moments are moments to grow in self-knowledge and humility.

4. We must trust that God is at work and that He is remarkably close to us in these moments. If we call out to Him, He will inspire us even if we do not sense His closeness – He is there at work!

The role of being the main lawgiver is a humbling one. One eats a lot of "humble pie." I have had to grow into this role. I have had to learn and unlearn what I received from my own experience of being fathered. It has been a process of what my spiritual director used to call moments of "tough graces." It is important to remember that when situations occur that are difficult moments, that all involved have something to see and to learn. We are all people in the process of being converted and needing healing.

Often, I do not look forward to such moments, but I have realized they are necessary for continued conversion. For then I must truly cry out to God the Father to father us in such "tough graced moments." I must humbly say that these times have become really gifts from God's hand. Just to realize this and see them as graced moments is what I call a "mega-gift."

The father as warrior/protector: This role is of particular importance from the ages of 12-18.

At this stage, the father needs to know how to fight for his children in two ways. "First, he needs to stand with them, fighting on their side as it were, confronting the confusing and frustrating changes that threaten to overwhelm both him and them. Second, he needs to fight against the forces that try to draw his children away from him or even place them in opposition to himself. Some of these forces come from the surrounding culture. Some arise from within the adolescent. Others arise from within the father. In order to fight for his children, the father must stay involved with them." [22]

At the heart of the warrior role is the father's ability to be willingly and courageously engaged in struggling on behalf of his children. The warrior father must channel his efforts on behalf of, and with, his children "so that he can actively engage and challenge them, but without always needing to win. He can take pleasure when his children master new skills – even when they surpass him." [23]

"If a father has been a good nurturer and a good lawgiver at earlier stages, his ability to be a warrior/protector at this

---

[22] Stoop, Ph.D., D. *Making Peace with Your Father*. Page 63.
[23] Ibid, Page 63.

point will launch his children into a healthy and fruitful adulthood." [24]

I believe at this stage the process of discernment of spirits is crucial. I must be able to trust what is moving me to protect my children. As in many things, we are learning and forming, and being formed by, the situations that God in His great wisdom allows. He has our best interests at heart. His purposes are holy and perfect even though they may seem very "messy."

I believe we must also maintain a listening heart. It is important in moments of even incredibly challenging difficulties, that we return to an inner Peace to be able to hear the voice of Jesus who always wishes to instruct and encourage. In moments of frustration, we MUST not allow the Enemy to sneak into our hearts and tell us, "You are useless" – or to accuse "You blew it!" Discouragement is one of the main signs the "father of lies" is close and at work. If we did indeed "blow it," we need to humbly admit it, repent and recover our peace as soon as is possible.

The father as spiritual mentor: This role is important as the child moves into adulthood.

---

[24] Ibid, Page 71.

Here I would like to point out a few things. St. Pope John Paul II spoke of his home as being his first seminary. His father was a good role model of a man of prayer, a man who sought always to please God. Here I would like to point out that it is tremendously beneficial if children see in their father an authentic witness to a life of prayer that is well balanced and rooted in reality.

We must avoid a life of faith that is disconnected from one's humanity. Instead, we must have a Christian spirituality that is not just a "head trip" but a "heart trip" as well. Children need to witness parents praying and playing together – and praying and playing together with them as well. This leads the family to bond with God and with each other.

When a family prays together eventually God begins to ask something of them. What might that be? To experience Jesus through a life of prayer opens our eyes to see Jesus in those whom society wishes not to see – the poor. What needs to be formed in family life is a spirituality that is Christ-centered (but includes the fullness of Christianity found in the Catholic Church); a spirituality that is warm and heart-felt. Not a spirituality that leads us away from our humanity to anything other than fully human, but that leads us to face our human condition and through His grace convert our humanity. If children see that prayer is normal and an important part of family life, they will bring this experience to the next generation as they begin their own families.

Jesus spent 30 of His 33 years at home. True Christian spirituality leads a parent to the heart of home life and to one's duties there. It has been said that no one could be so human as God.

This is what I believe – that an authentic life of prayer, a Sacramental life, study of Holy Scripture, adoration of the Blessed Sacrament, the rosary, etc., open us to becoming not only more human, but (even more importantly) to be parented by the Father – and then transformed by His grace. (More on this in a later chapter.)

A man who was never raised by an emotionally healthy father role model will likely find it more difficult to father his own sons or daughters in a healthy manner. If the man never experienced being the son of healthy father, fatherhood is an unknowable route, instead of a well-marked path that the man himself has journeyed before with his own father.

One must first heal – and grow up in the best sense of the word.

One must be free of one's past to be free for the future.

At a family gathering with my one and only Aunt Tula. She was like a mother to me…a living saint.

My parents, Frank and Rosa Scott.

During a family outing to a beach in Lima, Peru, sometime around 1964.

I am on the right, on the shoulders of my sister Lorraine. My twin brother Richard is on the left, on the shoulders of my sister, Margie.

Me at 15 years of age, with Whiskey, a family dog.

1989 – My ordination photo.

Me celebrating my First Mass, my Mass of Thanksgiving, on May 7, 1989. I was so nervous that my twin brother Richard had to point out every part of the Mass. Richard is to my immediate left (your right).

Me and my twin Richard (who goes by name of Father Martín as a priest), during the opening hymn at my Mass of Thanksgiving on May 7, 1989.

My twin, Father Martin, and I have celebrated many Masses together over the years. In June 2023, about a month after the 34th anniversary of my ordination, we celebrated Mass together at a conference in Springfield, Missouri.

I have had several German Shepherds over the years, and they have all been "very good boys."

This is my first German Shepherd, Moses, and me on Christmas Day, 1994.

Me, with my sister Lorraine and Maria, a friend of ours from Spain – together with members of the Catholic community in the slum "Vallecito," at our house in Naña, Peru.

Page 93

My community, Family of Jesus, and me at our yearly community retreat in January 2023 in Peru.

Chapter Five – The Heart of a Child Who Has not Experienced the Blessing

"Un-parented people do not know who they really are. They do not believe they are loveable – they live in anguish." – This book's Author

I have been working with families, children, adolescents and adults for most of my priesthood. If a family is not rooted in Godly love, the results are the same – whether the family is poor or well-to-do. When I meet men and women who have been un-parented, they have lived in a home where the Blessing was not given or just partly given. They long to be loved.

There is an anguish, a look in their eyes that communicates "Help, please help me." Often their faces (depending on the depth of their deprivation) are expressionless. If they are in groups, and others are sharing their own stories, they look off into space with a blank stare. They cannot focus on the pain or thirst of others to be loved, because their own hunger and thirst is too great and all-consuming. To hear, to really hear, others' anguish immediately reminds them of their own reality, both past and present. Without knowing it, they are very self-centered. Because no one has ever focused on them, they cannot help but focus on themselves. They fight for attention.

Life becomes a competition to be heard and noticed. A young woman will dress in a seductive way because she cries for a person to notice her. Her way of dressing shouts out "Look at me!" It is common for women who have not received this unconditional love, this Blessing, to become sexually active at an early age. In addition, "boyfriends" of these young women are often much older, perhaps because the young lady is seeking a father figure she never knew.

For some time two members of my community and I gave a yearly retreat for women who have had an abortion. During these retreats, as I listened to women's stories about their abortion(s), I learned from them that they never received the parental Blessing.

The greatest sexual organ is the human heart. When the Blessing does not form it, it becomes de-formed by a lifestyle spent looking for love wherever and however it can be found. As the heart falls deeper into its anguish, it falls deeper into fear and self-hatred, and suffers through repeated abandonments. Women without the Blessing have such de-formed hearts, have such loneliness and live in such self-hatred that when they become pregnant, they

feel their only/best option is to resolve or eliminate their problem. So, they abort.
I have met women on these retreats in Peru who have had up to ten abortions.

Only God really knows how culpable anyone is when he or she sins. So only God really knows how responsible a person is who lives a life of addiction, a life of safe-hatred, of loneliness – due to having a life not rooted in the Blessing of the parents. These poor women arrived at these retreats looking like "walking tombs."

God knows all, and He "tsunamis" them, overwhelming them with tidal waves of grace found in first facing the truth of choice, and then in their acceptance of His mercy.

He would then lead them in peeling back layer after layer of pain, ultimately revealing what is behind and underneath their choice of abortion – a home life without the Blessing. As each began to understand the mystery of her heart and accepted the truth of her heart's cry, she began to suffer with hope. Before, she suffered alone – now she suffered *with* someone, Jesus.

Her suffering could be beautifully described in the words of John 19:25, "Standing by the cross of Jesus [was] His mother…" Hope grows stronger in each of these women, as each realizes that the Blessed Mother is truly her

Mother too! Our Lady really wants to mother the woman, and the two of them work together to overcome the woman's choices that led to the destruction of the woman's life.

Once we unite our "cross" (our suffering) to Jesus' cross and to Jesus Himself, it becomes life giving. Indeed, where once we drowned in our sin and suffering, we now "drown" in the Mercy and Love of God. Nothing can stop this, not even the trauma of an abortion and all that it entails.

The tsunami of God's Love and Mercy, in truth, sets us free – making us able to face the reality of what was done, or not done, for us via the Blessing. We are led to life in God, and though we might still experience pain, we now know that this pain is a sign we are alive and not dead.

When I tell people who are in touch with their pain for the first time that they are more alive than before, they suddenly have an expression on their faces as if what I just said is a moment of epiphany – "I am more alive now than before."

The "dead" do not feel pain. Furniture and other inanimate objects do not feel pain. Again, the dead are not alive. We feel pain *because* we are alive. John 8:32 tells us "... the truth will set you free."

What are some other characteristics of a person who has lived in a home without receiving the Blessing? A child from whom the Blessing is withheld struggles with (and may easily feel overwhelmed by) feelings of resentment, anger, fear and feelings of insecurity, discouragement and even depression. A child who never received the Blessing consistently compares himself with others, and always unfavorably; and feels overwhelmed by life's events. Such feelings are common and well up often inside a heart deprived of the gift of the Blessing. One's own home does not feel like home, for one's poorly formed heart does not experience "Shalom," the peace, security and well-being that God intends for each of us.

As an excellent illustration of this point, General H. Norman Schwarzkopf, in his autobiography *It Doesn't Take a Hero*, described what it was like growing up in a home with an alcoholic mother –

> "I used to dread coming home at night. I'd go around the side of the house, where there was a window that looked into the kitchen. I'd stand in the dark and look inside and try to judge what kind of night it was going to be. Mom had a Jekyll and Hyde personality. When she was sober, she was the sweetest, most sensitive, loving and intelligent person

you ever met. But when she was drunk, she was a holy terror...When mom was drunk, a terrible meanness would come out, mostly in the form of personal attacks on my sisters...The small jabs would go on until she sensed she'd hit on something my sister was particularly sensitive about, and then she'd bore in until my sister broke down in tears." [25]

Let us now look briefly at some of the things that happen when one only receives part of the blessing.

Take, for example, divorce. In typical divorces, the mother will get custody of the children, with the father seeing the children on a regular basis. A father will often lavish the children with gifts and attention right after the divorce. Here we see what is commonly known as the "sugar-daddy" syndrome. Children might feel closer to their father at this point in their lives. Unfortunately, such attention is temporary. It is common that after two or three years fathers will see their children once a month. The contact has decreased.

Children will long for the blessing of the absent parent. The custodial (often single) parent who is "doing their best" to provide for the children often cannot afford to

---

[25] Schwartzkopf, Gen. N. *It Doesn't Take a Hero*. Page 19.

lavish gifts upon the children. It is important for parents considering a divorce to realize that the scars caused by a divorce are deep and long lasting.[26]

Here is an example of what can happen when one parent abandons his or her home and children. In Peru, 65% of children are abandoned by their fathers before they are born. Having lived in Peru, I can testify to that, as well as testify to the fact that to be abandoned by a parent can often be worse than losing them due to a death.

When a child is abandoned, the child consistently seeks the abandoning parent(s). Often this is experienced when the child thinks he got a glimpse of the parent in a crowded street or at an airport. The child runs to catch up with the glimpsed person only to be disappointed when the child realizes the glimpsed person is not the parent who abandoned the child. Instead, the child is facing a stranger.

A speaker at a conference on "displaced children" stated: "A father who deserts his family suddenly and never sees them again can leave a daughter forever afraid to allow herself to be vulnerable to a man, sure that he too will leave her…His daughter's resulting anger may give her

---

[26] Adult children of divorce or separation might find the resources and assistance of the Life-Giving Wounds, a Catholic ministry, a good source of help. The ministry website is https://www.lifegivingwounds.org.

trouble with men all her life. She may totally avoid men, or keep seeking the father she never had." [27]

We have just touched the surface of the reality that lives in the heart of a child who has not received the Blessing. The authors of *The Blessing* tell us what such children can become. On pages 152-155, we read of what a child might be vulnerable to becoming if the child does not work past the hurts and damage experienced from a childhood without the parent's Blessing.

Children can become the seekers, those who constantly seek intimacy but who can hardly tolerate it. They often feel a tremendous emotional lift during a courtship. However, after the marriage their previous lack of acceptance from parents leaves them uncomfortable in receiving intimacy from their spouse. They do not know how acceptance feels, and they are never satisfied. These seekers may struggle with believing in God's unconditional love due to the lack of this kind of love in their early lives.

Or children may become smotherers, those who suck all the energy and life out of a spouse, a friend, a child or a parish or church. They are so wounded by their past that

---

[27] Trent, Ph.D., J and Smalley G. *The Blessing.* Page 149, who in turn were quoting Rev. Stephen Lyon, "Loving Your Children God's Way," an unpublished message given in Dallas, TX in 1983.

they smother others with their un-met needs. Those who carry the emotional weight of the smothering person's un-met needs become tired and pull away. For the "wounded" smotherer, this inability of another to handle the burden of a smotherer's needs communicates to them "rejection." The smotherer fails to realize that his or her smothering drives people away, and that the smotherer has brought this pain on himself or herself.

Or children may become chronically angry. From *The Blessing*, we read, "As long as people are angry with each other they are chained to each other... They are never forgiven or forgotten. As a result, the rattle and chafing of emotional chains distract them from intimacy in other relationships." [28]

Children may become detached. Here a person detaches themselves emotionally or literally from others to prevent him or herself from ever being hurt again. Yet this often makes their wound worse. By keeping a friend or spouse at "arms-length," loneliness becomes part of their emotional diet day after day.

Children may be easily seduced. Such people look for the love not given in a Blessing in the wrong places. Here one tries to get lost love often in sexual immorality. Their cry for love is sought in unhealthy ways. As I wrote earlier

---

[28] Ibid. Page 153.

in this book, the human heart is our greatest sexual organ. If the heart is not fed in the right way, the person who has the malnourished heart will often seek an unhealthy way to meet the heart's need. Particularly astounding examples of this unhealthy seeking are found in a 2022 study, which outlines the results of research on Adverse Childhood Experiences (ACEs).

The study authors report in the introduction, "There is increasing evidence that adults with ACEs are at greater risk for diseases (e.g., alcoholism, myocardial infarction, stroke, depression, diabetes, and coronary heart disease) and disability due to health status. Moreover, ACEs are a major risk factor for drug abuse...Individuals with ACE scores ≥5 are seven to 10 times more likely to report illicit drug addiction compared to those without ACEs and are four to 12 times more likely to become drug abusers. In short, ACEs not only affect physical and mental health but also increase the risk of drug abuse in adulthood." [29]

However, there is real hope for healing here. We do not have to remain collapsed and crushed by a childhood where we did not receive the Blessing. Our personal

---

[29] He J, Yan X, Wang R, Zhao J, Liu J, Zhou C, Zeng Y. (2022) *Does Childhood Adversity Lead to Drug Addiction in Adulthood? A Study of Serial Mediators Based on Resilience and Depression.* Front Psychiatry. As defined in the study, "adverse childhood experiences (ACEs) are typically defined as stressful and/or traumatic experiences that occur during childhood."

"Good Friday" can be transformed to our own "Easter Sunday."

Let's look at how God works through His chosen children, using these people as instruments to finally impart God's Blessing into lives from where it was previously missing. Let's look now at how God "writes straight with crooked lines" by giving us His Blessing.

Chapter Six – God Brings His Missing Blessing to the Un-fathered Wounded

"Even if my father and mother forsake me, the LORD will take me in."

(Psalm 27:10 ESV)

God has put in our hearts the thirsting longing to be loved unconditionally. This thirst has not been satisfied in anyone who has not received the Blessing and who has not worked through and resolved his or her own issues. And with this thirst unsatisfied, those without the Blessing are not able to give the Blessing to anyone. You can only give what you have received.

Yet our Father still longs to impart the blessing even though a person did not receive it from parents. There is hope. We read in John 1:12-13, "But to those who did accept him he gave power to become children of God, to those who believe in his name, who were born not by natural generation nor by human choice nor by a man's decision but of God." God will still find a way to impart His blessing. Why? Because Love will find a way and God is love.

I met a religious sister who was "given away" as a baby. As the product of a street market is given away, she was given away. She grew up seeking the Blessing. One day at the age of seven she was incredibly sad and was hiding underneath a table, and did not want to come out. A priest friend of the family was asked to come to the house and try to talk to the young girl. The priest bent down underneath the table and began to speak to her. He convinced her to come to him and tell him what was wrong. The girl had found out that the couple she thought were her parents were not her biological parents. She was told she had been given away. He began to ask her questions and to listen to her. He began to spend time with her and to "father" her.

Today she says that priest became her father. She received the Blessing she never received from her parents through him.

We priests are called to become "spiritual fathers" for the un-parented, for those who have not received the Blessing.

That is why we are called "Father." In the book of Judges, we hear of a Levitical priest who is told by Micah,

> "Stay with me… Be father and priest to me…" (Judges 17:10).

A priest has received from God the Father a special mission, a call to reveal his Fatherhood in a prophetic way, in such times as these, when so many of God's children grow up un-parented.

I chose many years ago to seek counseling and let God heal my heart that had never known the Blessing. God placed in my life men who were very fatherly and men of integrity. One was Dr. Tom Byron, the veterinarian of my first German Shepherd. At the time I was pastoring my first parish, Our Lady of Guadalupe in Wimauma, Florida – a small town that seemed to have more than its share of the country's drug traffic.

This was my first experience ministering to the poor, and my first two-plus years at the mission were exceedingly difficult. During this time, all of the funerals I said were for men that had been shot to death due to their participation in the drug world. It was both heartbreaking and very frustrating to see wives and their children destroyed by the death of their husbands and fathers.

During this time, my friend Tom and I would eat breakfast together every Saturday morning. He would listen and encourage me. On one occasion, I got tired of burying men killed in the drug world, and out of my frustration, I broke a tennis racket with my bare hands.

Tom listened to me and got into my heart. Soon after I had broken my tennis racket, during our breakfast he took out a tennis racket. He had tears in his eyes. As our watering eyes connected, I experienced in my heart, "You understand my frustration. You really do understand." I cried as Tom gave me the racket. Tom became a "father" to me. He spoke to me about the religious community I felt called to found in order to heal the family. He would tell me, "Father, you must do this. The world needs this. It will one day be a reality."

Tom's words gave my heart wings.

After I began the community Tom got cancer. I went to his house to anoint him and prepare him for death. Tom knew he was going to die and that his death would be soon. He asked me to celebrate his funeral and to preach at it. I did. When I was preaching, I began to cry, and cried hard. Tom had been sent by God to impart the Blessing. I had buried my own father three years after my ordination to the priesthood, but I must tell you that I cried more at Tom's funeral than at my own father's.

No man is born knowing fatherhood – it is a gift acquired through example, practice, experience – and much, much prayer.

With time God put into my path other men as examples of what a father is to be. Also, as the years have passed God has put me into the path of countless children, adolescents and men and women whom I know God has fathered through me and imparted His Blessing through my priesthood. Young women have even asked my opinion of how they were dressed. Some girls have told their boyfriends, "I will not marry you until Father Philip checks you out, and I get his approval."

One girl who had lived for most of her life lacking the Blessing called me one day in Peru. I was going to go to Tampa and give a retreat, and she had heard I was coming. Although she lived around an hour away from where I would be, she told me, "Father, my birthday is coming up. I would like to give myself a gift. I want to have lunch with you. You are the father I never had." We talked and she told me of what it meant for her that God put me in her life as a "Father."

Sometime after this event, I received an e-mail from a young woman in Ecuador who asked me if I could "adopt" her as a spiritual daughter. This is a common "cry" in the heart of men and women of our day. As a priest I insist on being called "Father" for this very reason. Our world is largely unparented and full of people who have not received the Blessing.

In the next chapter, I share with you how God prepares the soil of our heart to be "fathered" by Him.

Chapter Seven – God Fathers Us by First Weakening Us

"It is true that the voice of God, having fully penetrated the heart, becomes strong as the tempest and loud as the thunder; but before reaching the heart it is weak as a light breath which scarcely agitates the air. It shrinks from noise, and is silent amid agitation."

– St. Ignatius of Loyola

When a person has not received the unconditional love found in what Scripture calls the Blessing, and receives a curse instead, the heart is in turmoil and the smallest "event" can agitate it. When one is not heard, noticed, appreciated, remembered and is misunderstood, the poor soul falls into turmoil and is tormented with thoughts of anger, discouragement, frustration – there is no peace.

In such moments, the voices of the past and other rejections become "too loud" and God seems to have left us as a victim-mouse in the paws of a cat. Each perception of misunderstanding and rejection sends the person into a tailspin, like a passenger in a one-engine plane spinning out of control just before the plane crashes. What can be done? How can we silence those thoughts that are often diabolical and are called "distorted thinking?"

When one has not been formed in the Blessing, one must face life's events alone because the father and mother have not been emotionally engaged in the "heart-mind" world of their child. There was a family who asked me to meet with them after I had finished a retreat in a beautiful Andean city in Ecuador. We began around midnight, and I asked the daughters if they wanted to tell their father anything. The youngest who was around eight years old suddenly broke out, "Dad, I'll bet you do not even know my favorite color!"

My dear reader, if you are a parent, I have a few questions to ask you. Do you know these things about your children? [30] These questions help us become "students" of our children, and we learn more about what is going on inside them.

    1.   What do they most often daydream about?

---

[30] Ibid. Page 117.

2. When they think of their years as young adults, (twenty to thirty years of age) what would they really enjoy doing?
3. Of all the people they have read about in the Bible (or saints) who is the person they would most like to be like and why?
4. What do they think God wants to them to do for humankind?
5. What type of boyfriend or girlfriend are they most attracted to, and why?
6. What is the best part of their school day and what part is the worst?

Did you have parents who knew this information about you? If the answer is "No," then our parents did not know that part of our world. My parents could not answer these questions. If we can basically say our parents did not know us, we could say in some ways we raised ourselves and faced much of what we questioned on our own. We had to become self-sufficient. But the fact is that we were not.

Did I experience my parents' eyes lighting up when I arrived home? In the book of Proverbs we read, "A cheerful glance brings joy to the heart..." (Prov 15:30). We can transform a person by the way we look at him or her. Did we ever see our parents' eyes tearing up with love just by looking at us?

Slawomir Biela, author of *God Alone Suffices*, begins the introduction to his highly esteemed book, "One of the basic human psychological needs is the need for security, the feeling that we are in control, that we can manage the situation. From a human point of view, it would be ideal if such a need was satisfied, however, then, we would no longer need God. After all, are we not the ones who can manage just fine on our own? Are we not in control of our own lives? It seems certain, then, that you are the *masters* of our own destinies." [31]

Such a perspective was not constructed overnight. A child may himself or herself create a "pseudo" philosophy on life to maintain his/her self-illusion of being in control. This was done daily when one could not rely upon or trust the parents to give him/her the security of living in a house where the Blessing was a total gift. There is hope, in that we must trust and believe that God wants to step in and parent us.

How does He begin to do this? The very fact that we can admit and face the truth that we were raised in a home with little unconditional love indicates that already God is at work.

---

[31] Biela, Slawomir. *God Alone Suffices*. Page xxxv.

Jesus the Divine Healer is different from a doctor in an operating room. The operating room doctor closes the wound with stitches. Jesus does the opposite, and begins His healing by *opening* the wound. The pain and emptiness we feel at the opening is the beginning of us receiving the Blessing. He is doing what St. Paul experienced when Paul asked God to remove the "thorn in the flesh." What did our Lord tell him? "My grace is sufficient for you, for power is made perfect in weakness." (2 Cor 12:9)

He was saying "I am all you need." God wanted to be everything for Paul. He wanted to parent him.

We must move from a self-reliance and a compulsion to solve all our situations, and instead let God's voice become "louder" than all the anxiety and agitation we feel when we face every new problem (including our process of conversion). How does He create this "dependence" upon Him and willingness to listen to Him? We must be weakened to see His power, to experience His Fatherhood.

Let us ask ourselves a question: "How much do I pray?" In Luke 6:12, we read that Jesus, being unfailingly in communion with His Father, spent the whole night in prayer. As man, His reason to be on earth was to do nothing more and nothing less than His Father's will. Period. If we pray little, we rely too much on ourselves to be "self-sufficient" – an utterly impossible task – as opposed to God being the One upon Whom we really MUST rely.

What are some ways we try to be "strong"? We do not seek help or advice from others and try to figure things out by ourselves alone. We have trouble admitting we are wrong when we really are. We have trouble showing our emotions and being vulnerable in front of others. We pray little if any at all. There is a Carmelite expression that if a "ball" is to rise "high," it must first hit "bottom." So also, we need to allow ourselves to hit rock bottom and be vulnerable if we are to be lifted and advance in the spiritual life.

Are you weak enough to live as a son or daughter of the Father? Simply speaking, we must let God be God. His Fathering is of another world, and He knows what He is doing. We do not! In Isaiah, the Lord tells the prophet, "For my thoughts are not your thoughts, nor are your ways my ways..." (Isa 55:8). As mentioned before in this book, God is what St. Thomas Aquinas called "pure act." He is ALWAYS working on our behalf! He is *never* **not** doing something or potentially about to do something.

Are we not told in Scripture that Our Eternal Parent "never tires or grows weary?" We see this process of needing to be weakened and to be guided in the life of Gideon. In Judges 7:1-7 we read,

> "Early the next morning Jerubbaal (that is, Gideon) encamped by the spring of Enharod with all his soldiers. The camp of Midian was in the valley north of Gibeath-hammoreh. The LORD said to Gideon, "You have too many soldiers with you for me to deliver Midian into their power, lest Israel vaunt itself against me and say, 'My own power brought me the victory.' Now proclaim to all the soldiers, 'If anyone is afraid or fearful, let him leave.' When Gideon put them to this test on the mountain, twenty-two thousand of the soldiers left, but ten thousand remained. The LORD said to Gideon, "There are still too many soldiers. Lead them down to the water and I will test them for you there. If I tell you that a certain man is to go with you, he must go with you. But no one is to go if I tell you he must not." When Gideon led the soldiers down to the water, the LORD said to him, "You shall set to one side everyone who laps up the water as a dog does with its tongue; to the other, everyone who kneels down to drink." Those who lapped up the water raised to their mouths by hand numbered three

hundred, but all the rest of the soldiers knelt down to drink the water. The LORD said to Gideon, "By means of the three hundred who lapped up the water I will save you and will deliver Midian into your power. So let all the other soldiers go home."

Imagine the scene. The Midianites have an army of 125,000 strong, and they are not "patsies." Gideon did not want to lead the Israelites into this fight. He tries to get himself out of it by making sure (really sure) God is asking this of him. After all, Israel faces being outnumbered four to one by the Midianites. Moreover, as God prepares Gideon and Israel's army for the attack God does something that seems absurd. He weakens Gideon and his army from 32,000 to 300.

Things seem to be worse, but this is the Wisdom of God. St. Paul realized this. To the Corinthians he writes, "'…for power is made perfect in weakness.' I will rather boast most gladly of my weaknesses, in order that the power of Christ may dwell with me. Therefore, I am content with weaknesses, insults, hardships, persecutions, and constraints, for the sake of Christ; for when I am weak, then I am strong." (2 Cor 12:9-10)

Let us look again at the pages of *God Alone Suffices*. In the introduction we read, "Through inner inspirations, through His continuous showering of you with His uncountable graces, through emotional experiences or spiritual dryness, God will want to convince us existentially that we are not, and we cannot be, the masters of our destinies.

It is He who is the only *Kyrios*, the only Master. He will want to convince us that the faith and hope we have in ourselves are illusory like any other fiction. They ARE GOING (emphasis mine) to fall apart, and He is the one who will mercifully heal our wounds resulting from this process. He will try to convince us that He loves us more than life – that we are His adopted sons and daughters, who are created out of nothingness." [32]

I had no idea God had in mind to teach me how close He is to us and how much I truly need Him as Father, as protector.

My community and I arrived in Peru on January 10, 2003. I had just bought a truck to help drive and work in the bad terrain of the slum outside of Lima. Roughly three months had passed and it was the feast of St. Louis-Marie de Montfort. I was headed into Lima to meet a young man who was interested in the community. When I was heading off the main road, I noticed on the exit ramp a car

---

[32] Ibid. Page xxxix.

stopped. It seemed like someone was experiencing car trouble.

As I paused and stopped, suddenly four men came out of the car with guns loaded and screaming, "Get out of the car." I told them, "Here are the keys. You can keep the truck." They yelled, "No, we want you. I looked behind my truck and there was another car full of armed men. At least nine or ten highly armed men surrounded me. I insisted that they take the truck, but was struck twice on my head by the butt of a gun and pushed out of my truck – while the hood of my habit covered my head. Some of the men forced me into the backseat of one of their vehicles. They pressed guns into my head and I was told, "If you try anything or say anything, we will kill you."

My body was in "shock" mode. It took me around four to five minutes to admit the fact that I had been kidnapped. But this was no April Fool's joke. However, after I accepted the truth that I was kidnapped I told Jesus, "You have prepared me for this moment all my life." Every fiat, every "Yes" of my will had prepared me to say "Yes" at this moment in my life. "Yes – with all my heart and I offer my life for you," I told Jesus. I was keenly aware this was a moment to embrace, no matter what was to be the final outcome.

Suddenly I was aware of a peace in me, and all around me. My thinking was clear, and I was not afraid. I prepared myself to die if it was my Eternal Father's will. He had foreseen this event from all eternity, and I was not in control. But I experienced a security, a deep sense of God's closeness. I was completely out of control of my life – but God was in control instead.

During my kidnapping turmoil, and after more than two hours of internal prayer, I had finished doing an examination of my whole life. I renewed my commitment to God and asked once again forgiveness for the sins of my whole life. Suddenly I was taken into my spirit, my deepest "me," and I experienced a bright light that I cannot even begin to describe. I'm not sure if I was taken to Heaven, or if Heaven came down to me, but I knew I was home.

I felt the Presence of the Blessed Trinity, as I was engulfed in a totality of love, acceptance and belonging that I had never known. Then these words of knowledge – not spoken, but nevertheless there around, in front of, behind, all around me – something like "My son, what separates you and Us is a thread. Time and eternity." I knew deeply that if I was executed, I would be immediately in my Father's arms. My home! My home!!

It seemed to me as if I were dancing on one foot in my heart. All was well because I knew – really knew – that God was closer to me than I was to myself. My kidnappers continued driving. Around an hour later without rehearsing any prepared "script," these words came out of my mouth, "My brothers, I want you to know that I forgive you." The gentleman in whose lap I was resting my hooded head said to me, "Father, please pray for me." I was shocked at the words that had exploded out of my mouth, as I had not even been thinking them.

Around ten minutes later the same words came out of my mouth again, "My brothers, I want you to know that I forgive you." I was shocked once again. And around five minutes later the same words came out of my mouth a third time, "My brothers, I want you to know that I forgive you," but this time I shouted the words with a God-given authority.

They were as shocked as I was. They kept driving and turned onto a road surrounded by only empty desert. The car stopped and I thought to myself, "Here is my moment to die for Christ." They told me to get out of the car and to not look back. However, I planned to turn around and fully expected to hear gunfire that would end my earthly life, as I extended my arms in the form of a cross and cried out the words, "Viva Cristo Rey!"

Suddenly and surprisingly, the gunmen changed their minds about killing me and sped off quickly – leaving me alone in the middle of desert area.

Later that year, during my silent priest retreat, Jesus brought up the event of the kidnapping and said to me, "They were going to execute you, but I intervened." I said, "When did you that?" I then heard His answer, "When you shouted three times, 'My brothers, I want you to know that I forgive you.'" The gunmen were armed and the Holy Spirit disarmed them by the "power and authority" that came from those words of forgiveness.

I share with you, my dear reader, my story of almost being executed so that you may see more clearly that we are not the owners of our lives. God is. We are God's and He can ask of us whatever He wants. He knew what the outcome would be.

I must admit I was disappointed that I had not been killed. In fact, I was angry and depressed for two days. On the third day, I "made up" with Him. What happens in your life hopefully causes you to begin to realize, "I have no control." Your crises are what God uses to weaken YOU! Realize that you need Him and Him alone.

Again, we turn to the powerful book *God Alone Suffices*, "If we are still capable and strong in certain areas of our lives, we need to acknowledge that this is only a temporary state. Being in good physical condition, being in good spirits psychologically, or being in great 'spiritual condition' (our own perception) – all this is fleeting. Everything gradually must be taken away from us some day so that we can cling only to God. Our powerlessness and a sense of total dependence on our Creator in all areas of our lives should become a norm for us – when we are completely permeated by the words of Jesus who said: 'Without me you can do nothing.' (John 15:5) **Nothing** – this means not even the smallest thing." [33]

In the next chapter we will spend some time with the idea that God has given us a "thirst" for the Eternal, and that – apart from God – no person, place or thing will ever satisfy the immensity of that thirst and hunger. However, we can touch the place where only He Who is Uncreated can satisfy our created being. No *human* Blessing, even from the best of parents, could quench the insatiable thirst that has been placed in us by God.

---

[33] Ibid. Pages 62-63.

Chapter Eight – Jesus: The Only Son – to Whom Does He Reveal the Father?

Before I address my personal encounter with the Father, whom I affectionately call "Papa," let's review the late Pope Benedict XVI's treatment of Jesus as "the Son." An experience of a creature as a "son" or a "daughter" comes not by nature (as we by nature are not Divine like Jesus), but through adoption experienced in baptism. It is a gift granted by God through baptism that we share in His filial relationship with the Father.

Jesus is by nature the Son of God. Jesus ALONE is the Son. Pope Benedict XVI in his book *Jesus of Nazareth* wrote,

> "...Only the Son truly 'knows' the Father. Knowing always involves some sort of equality....Every

process of coming to know something includes in one form or another a process of assimilation, a sort of inner unification of the knower with the known…Truly to know God presupposes communion with Him, it presupposes oneness of being with him…

"'No one has ever seen God; it is only the Son, who is nearest to the Father's heart, who has made him known.' (John 1:18) …Only the Son knows the Father, and all real knowledge of the Father is a participation in the Son's filial knowledge of him, a revelation that he grants. ('He made him known,' John tells us.) …

"But to whom does the Son will to reveal him? The Son's will is not arbitrary. What we read in Matthew 11:27 about the Son's will to reveal the Father brings us back to the initial verse 25, where the Lord thanks the Father for having revealed knowledge to the little ones." [34]

"The Son wills to draw into his filial knowledge all those whom the Father wills should be there. This is what Jesus means when he says in the bread of life discourse at Capernaum, 'No one can come to

---

[34] Ratzinger, Joseph (Pope Benedict XVI). *Jesus of Nazareth*. Pages 340-341.

me unless the Father who sent me so wills...' (John 6:44). But who does the Father will? Not 'the wise and understanding.' the Lord tells us, but the simple.

"Taken in the most straightforward sense, these words reflect Jesus' actual experience: It is not the Scripture experts, those who are professionally concerned with God, who recognize Him; they are too caught up in the intricacies of their detailed knowledge. Their great learning distracts them from simply gazing upon the whole, upon the reality of God as he reveals himself – for people who know so much about the complexity of the issues, it seems it just cannot be so simple." [35]

There is a process to become "simple" and "un-wise" in the eyes of others and ourselves. The Son of God, Jesus, reveals the Father to those who know they are of no account. They know they are "nothing to write home about." They have eaten "humble pie" – and often!

Pope Benedict goes on to quote St. Paul who stated, "Let no one deceive himself. If anyone among you thinks that he is wise in this age, let him become a fool that he may become wise." (1 Cor 3:18) Then Pope Benedict asks, "What, though, is meant by 'becoming a fool,' by being 'a

---

[35] Ibid. Pages 341-342.

little one,' through which we are opened up for the will, and so for the knowledge, of God?" [36]

What allows us to "see?" This "seeing" is the opposite condition of which Jesus spoke when He stated, "they look but do not see and hear but do not listen or understand." (Matt 13:13) What is needed to see and be able to enter into the relationship that Jesus shares with His Father?
Pope Benedict related the answer to this question by quoting Matthew 5:8, "Blessed are the pure of heart, for they shall see God," and then he continues "Purity of heart is what enables us to see. Therein consists the ultimate simplicity that opens our life to Jesus' will to reveal. We might also say that our will has to become a filial will. When it does, then we can see...." [37]

A "pure heart" is, as the Church Fathers wrote, a "single heart." We must be "single-hearted." Our heart's sole desire must be all for God and God alone.

We must become "like children." We must become "little" in our eyes. This takes time. In our culture we want everything fast. We want to be healed quickly, like a problem revealed at the beginning of a three-hour movie that is solved by the movie's end. God does not work like that, though He could if He wanted. It takes time mixing

---

[36] Ibid. Page 342.
[37] Ibid. Page 343.

with eternity (Mass, prayer and suffering) – we must be weakened.

Earlier I wrote using the example of Gideon, who was told by God that he and the Israelites were too many – too strong. (Even though the Midianite army had four times as many soldiers as the Israelite army!) We must be "cut down to size." However, how big we are in our own eyes does not matter. How big we are – how strong we are according to our own point of view – is insignificant.

What matters is that we become humble, recognizing that we depend upon God for everything – and that we come to trust Him in everything. For instance, prayer before the Blessed Sacrament in adoration may seem to be a waste of time, a kind of "holy foolishness" – yet this is exactly what we need to do to grow in humility and toward an ever-closer relationship with Our Lord Jesus.

How surprised are you when you sin? How long does it take for you to "recover" your composure when you fall or make a "fool" of yourself in the sight of those to whom you admire. We must be formed in the school of "holy foolishness" and become weak – and become "fools" for Christ. This must happen if we are to grow as sons and daughters of the Father. This is for most of us, and including myself, a long and heart-wrenching process. That is what the whole process of conversion is all about, "baby." As John the Baptist so clearly stated in John 3:30, "He must increase; I must decrease."

What are some of the signs a person is decreasing, that a person is coming "down to size?" I would like to share some ways that I have slowly come to discover, by "falling" often only to get up again and again. The Father has put me into a life and ministry among the poor – from the streets of Ybor City in Tampa, to being amidst migrant workers in Wimauma, Florida, to living and working among the poor in Peru.

The poor have become my teachers. They are not "learned" as the world would define a "learned" person. Indeed, the poor have lived for so long at the bottom of society that it may be to some surprising and outright astonishing that the poor ARE lifted high – but not in the eyes of the rich and powerful. The poor are lifted high in the eyes of the only and truly Wise One, our God.

The perspective of Jesus is true: "The last shall be first." [38] The poor have no "fans" or "followers." They are not asked for autographs. They are not considered "influencers," nor do many people want to be "like" the poor. They are usually "last" on people's Christmas gift or card lists, if they appear on the lists at all. In Peru, the

---

[38] This phrase actually appears four times within the Gospels - Matthew 19:30; 20:16; Mark 10:31, and Luke 13:30.

wealthy feel they have "done something" for the poor because they participate in "Chocolatadas." [39]

However, the truth of the matter is that no man, even a poor one, lives on bread alone (or on "chocolatadas") because ALL men, the poor and wealthy alike, have dreams and needs. The poor parents stay up at night worrying about the present and future of their children. Poor people want to and dream of getting out of the slums for a better future. They tell me they feel God is angry at them. But they do not know why. The world in general seems "against" them. Maybe not in theory, but effectively so as evidenced by lacks and gaps in practical assistance to them.

People that "have" wear "blinders," so they will not be forced to see those that "cry out" day and night to their heavenly Father for justice. I literally have seen the poor looking through the windows of Burger Kings in Lima, Peru as others enjoy their meals inside. For the poor to eat in a McDonald's or Burger King is a luxury. Also, I have witnessed the managers of these fast-food restaurants tell those who are looking in to leave because they are not

---

[39] The Chocolatada is an eagerly anticipated annual event and longstanding Peruvian Christmas tradition. Every December, local organizations, companies, and municipal governments give out panetón – a bread-like cake with dried fruit), toys, and enormous pots of hot chocolate to Peru's rural and disadvantaged communities.

good for their business. Those that "have" wear blinders, but God does not!

I once had a dream, which I believe was from God, which told me to open my ministry to the wealthy, for they too needed to be evangelized. I did. When I have spoken to them during Bible studies about the poor, their facial expressions change. It is as if they were telling me, through these wordless expressions, "Teach us about anything, but stop making us uncomfortable." These people go to prayer groups and even daily Mass. But for many, visiting where the poor live and learning to truly "see" the poor is not on their radar screens.

I know a wonderful woman in Guayaquil, Ecuador, I'll call "Juanita." She wanted to work among the poor. The priest who was her spiritual director said to her, "[Juanita], I think I found the perfect place for you to begin your ministry to the poor." He took her to a place where the "chamberos" (those who live among the large piles of trash outside the city) live. As they arrived, the priest and Juanita stepped out of their car to look at the "mountains" of trash everywhere. Suddenly, in front of them, they noticed the trash begin to move like a whirlpool, as if a chambero was trying to get out from under this mountain of trash.

And yes, there was such a man! This man revealed himself slowly from under the trash and said to her, "[Juanita], welcome! I have been waiting. I have been waiting for you." It was Jesus, disguised as a chambero.

The great philosopher Pascal, when he was on his death bed, would ask for a beggar to be brought to his bedside to sit with him. Pascal could no longer receive the Eucharist, so he would ask for what was most like Jesus – the poor – to visit him.

What are other qualities of the "pure of heart?" Their flaws are very apparent to them, and they do not make excuses for themselves. For example, they just tell you the awful way they treated their child. They are transparent. Another sign is that they ask for help. They do not imagine themselves or act as if they are strong. They know they are not. They beg from what they need to the point of being a pain, and do not feel ashamed.

I am reminded of the widow in Luke's gospel whom Jesus spoke about. We read in Luke 18,

> "'because this widow keeps bothering me, I shall deliver a just decision for her lest she finally come and strike me.' And the Lord said, "Pay attention to what the dishonest judge says. Will not God then secure the

rights of his chosen ones who call out to him day and night?'" (Lk. 18:5-7)

Such "little ones" cry out to God. Their prayer comes up from their "bowels," from their guts. It takes time to move from a prayer that resides "up in our heads" (prayer on purely an intellectual level) to prayer that has comes from "way down" – from deep in our guts (from the depths of the soul).

Another sign of a pure heart is that such people admit their faults and shortcomings quickly because they have come to realize that they are nothing without God. So, when they are wrong, it does not take a long time for them to admit it. They recognize their errors and are even grateful to see their weaknesses and flaws. We see this in the life of St. Paul (see 2 Cor 12) and St. Theresa of the Child Jesus. They are not what is "important." They want the truth even if they must see or be shown repeatedly their errors, flaws and sin.

Yes, this is what it takes – and it takes seeing repeatedly, for we do not see very easily our flaws and sinfulness. Recognizing and acknowledging our errors, weaknesses and flaws improves our spiritual eyesight. Pope Saint Paul VI taught that to rediscover God we must rediscover our sin. Often, we must experience just how wrong we can truly be and have been to at last more clearly see the truth.

I am reminded of David when God sent Nathan to expose his sin. Nathan told David a parable about a rich man who took the only little lamb a poor man had to feed a friend of his – even though all the while the rich man had many sheep to choose from to feed his guest. As he listened to this story, David became furious and shouted,

> "As the LORD Lives, the man who has done this merits death!" (2 Sam 12:5)

Nathan then told David the hard truth,

> "You are the man!" (2 Sm. 12:7)

How this must have cut David down to size! David had been so successful in battle and popular as a King, but he did not live in the truth of what sin he had committed in ensuring Uriah's death. David's reaction to Nathan's parable must also happen in us. The truth must cut into us – as deeply as needed for us to see and feel it.

Saint Mother Teresa of Calcutta used to remind her sisters that she feared more her successes than her failures. This becoming in touch with our "littleness" is what allows us to realize that we must put all our eggs in God's basket, and none in our own. Our basket is weak and full of holes.

A person who sees his weaknesses and shortcomings, his littleness, begins to take himself/herself less seriously.

St. Lawrence called the poor the "the treasures of the Church." Do we see the poor this way, or truly as our teachers? Are we willing to be taught to see by those that are of "no account?" If we are not already seeing the poor this way, we must first see how blind we are, and take steps to improve and correct our sight. This "surgery" is long and painful. As our vision clears and brightens, we begin to see better and it becomes less painful.

We must see that we really are not what counts. It is God...God is ALWAYS the One who counts. And He has not hesitated to remind me of this when I need the reminder. Once when giving a retreat to priests, in the middle of my talk, it was as if someone unplugged me. All at once, I was absolutely incapable of saying even one more word. So, my talk ended with me simply making the sign of the cross. I left the room asking myself interiorly, "What just happened?!" In prayer the next morning, I asked God the Father what had happened during this talk. His answer came back quickly – resounding loudly – "Do you really think I need you?"

One more – as I am full of examples of my absolute nothingness...During one of my trips to Spain, one morning I had intended to concelebrate at daily Mass, but had not arrived at the Church in time to vest before Mass began, and so was sitting in the pews with a friend. After Mass, two women approached me, and one asked, "Are you Padre Felipe Scott? I said I was. She replied, "Oh, we follow you on YouTube."

I tried to downplay this, and an instant later, the Lord told me, "It was not you they were coming to see, but Me."

Rather, when we acknowledge that we fall by admitting we do not see, we find ourselves often in the confessional. This becomes a place that is familiar, and it is there we meet Jesus, who is slowly but surely choosing to reveal Himself as Mercy.

At first this "seeing" is still too much about us, but little by little we realize it really is about Him. At the same time, we must live for a while in the truth, that "I am not worthy to receive You." Saying that we are "not worthy" is not a "pity party" or just "mere words that are spoken" before communion time during Mass. Living the truth that we are not worthy is a slow but deep experience of being lifted from the reality of ourselves (our inner poverty) as being addicted to sin.

There is a grace that develops in a heart that sees its brokenness and is no longer shocked. It is to begin to experience what St. Paul calls the "freedom" of the children of God. We move from the poverty of our brokenness to the reality and wealth of His mercy. We begin to know – really know – we deserve hell. But all thanks and praise to Him, we have been saved from hell!

All is gift, all is grace and all is due to His mercy! However, moving from poverty of brokenness to wealth of Mercy is painful!

I call such moments "ouch moments." Why do they hurt? Because we really do not realize how poor in spirit we really are. We think and even act as if we are doing God a favor by praying, going to Mass and being "religious." We might attend Mass or "worship services" to gain or experience a sense of belonging, or to be faithful to our duties as a good citizen.

The fact is, we NEED to go to Mass or worship services because we need to remain in Him. Otherwise, we slowly but surely self-destruct. Our world is full of people who have done it "their own way" and find themselves empty and involved in a way of life that entices, pushes and pulls them to self-destruction. We think we are self-sufficient. We believe we really know best what is good for us and what will make us happy.

And the world affirms this lie with its "you do you" philosophy. So, we sin, and we sin a lot. How blind we are!

Did not Jesus say, "What profit would there be for one to gain the whole world and forfeit his life?" (Matt 16:26)

Let us hear Our Lord tell the Church in Laodicea, who thought they were really the church to be looked up to:

> "... For you say, 'I am rich and affluent and have no need of anything,' and yet do not realize that you are wretched, pitiable, poor, blind, and naked. I advise you to buy from me gold refined by fire, so that you may be rich, and white garments to put on so that your shameful nakedness may not be exposed, and buy ointment to smear on your eyes so that you may see." (Rev 3:17-18).

These changes are painful. However, they are also unbelievably valuable gifts that expose our pride, even though this pride may have been hidden by many masks.

And truly well-hidden is this pride of ours! Our true spiritual poverty to us may look like "riches." But this is a lie! Our lies to ourselves and about ourselves have become our identity, and must be torn away and exposed, so we might be "naked" enough to be clothed by the "garments" of His righteousness. Our Lord spoke of the need to lose our life to be able to save it. We must "lose" what we most value, so that we may find what Our Lord most values – a relationship that is "for real" with Him.

But we do not like to lose anything! In college football games, it is common for the winning teams to run out into the field with forefingers pointing up as if to say, "We are #1!" That will not do in the spiritual life if we really desire to meet the Father. If you are a person born in the 1950s or 1960s, I tell you, this attitude is not "cool" in the Father's eyes. If you were an adolescent after that, it might be better for me to tell you that this attitude most definitely is NOT "awesome."

The only one really cool or awesome thing is to allow God to be God in our lives! "Coke is [not] the real thing" – God – Father, Son, and Holy Spirit – is. We are talking about a Divine Family here, which you and I are called to know and to enter into and experience on this side of eternity.

Chapter Nine – My Encounter with the Father, My Papa

God allows, in those who never felt and were not given the Blessing, a set of experiences that must be repeated often. People I have met who had tasted an intimacy with God the Father, the Eternal Parent, speak of constantly living experiences of being misunderstood, isolated and lonely. To experience being "at home" in their homes would have meant receiving the Blessing, for Home is a place of the heart.

God often allows such souls to live a continual and a repeated reality of feeling isolated, misunderstood, and lonely. In this way, the Father prepares our heart, the "soil" of our being to be open to know, allow to grow, harvest and taste the Fatherhood of God. We must come to grips with the fact that these three repeated living conditions of loneliness, isolation and misunderstanding are meant (!) to move us; to nudge us toward our Eternal Parent, God the Father.

In other words, we must realize that these distasteful experiences were necessary in God's plans to move us from being "me-focused" to focusing on Him – and that these three types of painful experiences were the "stuff" that God the Father uses to open us up to Him. They make us look outside of this world's so-called "solutions" to an answer that only seems "out of this world" – God.

Even if my father and mother forsake me, the LORD will take me in.
(Ps. 27:10 ESV)

Well, we have now reached the place where we must stop blaming our parents for where we are in our lives. We must stop blaming our parents for "failing us" to whatever degree that occurred. We cannot make them responsible for our sins and mistakes. God allowed it and if God is God – and He most assuredly is – then He will somehow use it for His purposes. In Romans 8 we read,

> "We know that all things work for good for those who love God, who are called according to his purpose." (Rom 8:28)

His purpose is often hidden and we must wait to discover it through prayer that is founded on hope. God is good and He is about something – He is about a work in you. But what about understanding our part in that something? For me, as for most of us in similar situations, that "work" of God's had many layers.

First, I needed to make peace with my father.

A feather brings about the reconciliation with my father – God's grace, the supernatural, builds on the natural.

My Eternal Parent, my Papa, knew I needed to be reconciled to my biological parent. This was necessary, a must. So how did this happen? I was 22 years old, and I knew my relationship with my dad was not good. I had not even spoken to him about my entrance into the seminary. One morning as I was praying, a memory, an image, came to my mind. I saw myself on a beach in Peru looking for feathers. My father would have us, his children, look for feathers so we would tickle him in the back of his neck. In the memory, I was around seven years old. I thought to myself "It has been a long time since I tickled my father with a feather." I said a quick prayer. It went something like this "Lord, if you are asking me to tickle my dad with a feather, You are going to have to find me one."

In Peru, the beaches were close (Lima is on the coast of Peru), but now I lived over three hours from the closest one. And that was that. I continued my day, and right before dinner, I went to get my Bible. My Bible was well used (I read it daily) and was falling apart. When I opened the drawer of the night table, I found on my Bible a big, beautiful feather. But I knew the feather had not been there in the morning, so I believe an angel put it there.

That evening, I sat next to my father and tickled his neck with the feather as we watched a movie, and then the news, together with members of my family. I do not know what he was thinking as I did this for a LONG time.

Yet, my Papa God knew, and knew well. My father's heart was being softened for a "conversation" that I had tried to initiate with him right after my conversion experience. I had tried to ask my father's forgiveness for having rebelled during my adolescent years. My attempt led to a "sermon" by my dad naming all my past mistakes, flaws and saying basically that I "was amounting to nothing."

This new effort was my Papa's idea. It was His timing and method, placing a feather in my room – yes, sending me into "battle" with a feather as my weapon, even as I feared my new attempt to be reconciled with my father would once again end up in an argument. Again, this was God's idea and not mine. When the movie finished, we watched the news as a family and as that ended, my family, except for my father, went to bed. The two of us were left alone.

I said a prayer under my breath and spoke these words to my dad, "Dad, I need to talk with you." His first reply was, "Is it to tell me you are entering the seminary?" I said, "Well that is true, but that is not the reason." And I continued, "I need to ask your forgiveness for having rebelled so many times. I ask your forgiveness for having hated you and for wishing you dead. Please forgive me."

My father said, "I was too rough with you." The moment I heard, "I was too rough with you," I fell into his arms and started to kiss him all over his face. I cried and cried. I hung on to him. My father was stunned and could not talk. For me to hear those words was enough.

When you are starving, especially for something as important to your well-being as the love of a father, a little love goes a long way. We sat and talked for around 20 minutes – "heart to heart" for the first time ever. When we were done, my father stayed there by himself and sat in his chair in the dark.

Later, mother told me that she came downstairs to check on him wondering why he had not come upstairs to bed. She told me the next day, "I found your father alone and in the dark wiping tears away." Here I was, 22 years old, about to enter the seminary and I had just witnessed the "power" of a feather to move hearts and men to tears, when that feather was used as inspired by the Holy Spirit.

This event was necessary to prepare my heart's "soil" for its future harvest. I learned that asking for (and giving) forgiveness is necessary for the Father to lead us. Unforgiveness only creates more "noise" that muffles His voice in our souls and our lives. It is the door the Enemy uses to create what is called distorted thinking or, as my spiritual director calls it, "stinking thinking."

Is there unforgiveness in your heart? What thoughts are raised or come up when the topic of your father or mother or anyone else who has hurt you arises? What feelings are stirred up in you? If I remain with an unforgiving heart, I remain enslaved to the negative thoughts and memories associated with the person, which become quite a heavy burden to carry around and that only keep me from joy that might be otherwise mine from the Father. Please remember the part of the Our Father which Jesus gives to the apostles in Matthew 6:14-15, "If you forgive others their transgressions, your heavenly Father will forgive you. But if you do not forgive others, neither will your Father forgive your transgressions."

To forgive another is not to deny the hurt that the other has done to you or me. In fact, I would say that if we are to truly live, in a healthy way, the process of suffering in our lives, we must allow ourselves to really feel our pain and not just act like it was "really nothing" or "not important," when in fact the hurt to us was real.

There are wounds (whether physical, emotional, spiritual – perhaps even all three) that take time to heal. And during that time, we are taught not by books but by the Holy Spirit – in a way that is beyond words. We are taught the "wisdom of the cross." There are lessons to be learned, but only by working through them, including (at times) crying and screaming over these trials and their accompanying experiences. In the book of Hebrews 5:7, Jesus "offered prayers and supplications with loud cries and tears to the one who was able to save him from death, and he was heard because of his reverence."

In a real way, these are some of life's "goldmines," containing treasures hidden underneath many tears. From heaven's perspective the lessons are what move us towards holiness. I remember that during the process of founding a religious community, I came to realize it is a task literally impossible for a person to accomplish – humanly impossible that is. Honest truth.

In moments of trials and tears (and there were many) my spiritual director would say, "Do not waste this suffering." Truer words could never have been said. It was in such moments of suffering that it was an act (or acts) of forgiveness which often got the ball rolling.

No, it is not easy to forgive. For this we will need the assistance of Pope Benedict XVI. In his book, *Jesus of Nazareth,* he discusses the topic of forgiveness and "a price" that must be paid. While discussing the fifth petition of the Lord's prayer, "Forgive us our trespasses, as we forgive those who trespass against us...," Pope Benedict writes "...How to overcome guilt is a central question for every human life; the history of religions revolves around this question. Guilt calls for retaliation. The result is a chain of trespasses in which the evil of guilt grows ceaselessly and becomes increasingly inescapable. With this petition, the Lord is telling us that that guilt can be overcome only by forgiveness, not by retaliation. 'God is a God who forgives because he loves his creatures; but forgiveness can only penetrate and become effective in one who is himself forgiving.'" [40]

Pope Benedict continues, "If we want to understand the petition fully and make it our own, we must go one step further and ask: What is forgiveness, really? What happens when forgiveness takes place? Guilt is a reality, an objective force; it has caused destruction that must be repaired. For this reason, forgiveness must be more than

---

[40] Ratzinger, Joseph (Pope Benedict XVI). *Jesus of Nazareth.* Page 157.

a matter of ignoring, of merely trying to forget. Guilt must be worked through, healed, and overcome." [41]

We can count on forgiveness exacting a price from the person who forgives. The forgiver must "overcome within himself the evil done to him, as it were, burn it interiorly and in so doing renew himself. As a result, the forgiver also involves the other, the trespasser, in this process of transformation and inner purification; and both parties, suffering all the way through and overcoming evil, are made new. At this point, we encounter the mystery of Christ's cross." [42]

However, let's push 'Pause' in this discussion first. During the process of coming to forgiveness, we confront the limit of our power to heal or to overcome evil. Evil is a superior power (to us, though obviously not to God), and we cannot master it with our unaided powers – we CANNOT master it without God. "Reinhold Schneider says apropos of this that 'evil lives in a thousand forms; it occupies the pinnacles of power... it bubbles up from the abyss. Love has just one form – Your Son.'" [43]

---

[41] Ibid. Page 158.
[42] Ibid. Pages 158-159.
[43] Schneider, Reinhold. *Das Vaterunser*, page 68 – as quoted by Ratzinger, Joseph in *Jesus of Nazareth*, Page 159.

Schneider reminds us that the cost paid when one forgives falls on the one who forgives and not on the one who is being forgiven. Admittedly this can be (and often is) difficult to accept. That there is a cost to be paid by the forgiver, when the forgiver may have had NOTHING to do with causing or committing the trespass in the first place, may not only seem difficult, but rather unjust and backwards.

However, we must only look at the life of Jesus to see the Truth of this matter. It did not just cost Him to forgive you and me. It cost Jesus A LOT. **It cost Him EVERYTHING!** Jesus' forgiveness of us cost Him tremendous pain and torture and ended in His death on the cross. Given His example, we cannot expect another way. Forgiveness is GIVEN and not earned.

Forgiveness is free from the forgiver. I, We, must choose to forgive. You might be saying to yourself, "You do not understand. My father and mother did terrible things to me. And they never even said, 'Forgive us.'" My father never said those exact words either. Yet I knew I needed to be reconciled with him *for my sake*. In forgiving my father I was set free of all the hurt he had committed against me. My forgiveness of my father was an act of love – not just towards my father, for in forgiving my father I was learning to love myself.

Plus, God had forgiven me so much. In Matthew 18:21, Peter asks Jesus a question, "Lord, if my brother sins against me, how often must I forgive him? As many as seven times?" I wonder if Peter wanted to be named as the "poster child" of forgiveness. Prior to Jesus' public life, the people had learned from the law, which taught, "An eye for an eye, and a tooth for a tooth."

So, one hearing "As many as seven times?" from Peter might have expected to hear Jesus' reply "Peter, I am impressed. You are something else. I name you, "Mr. Forgiveness." Instead, Our Lord's reply to Peter was "I say to you, not seven times but seventy-seven times." (Matt 18:22) Peter must have thought, "Say what? Seventy times?... what?"

Considering that the symbolism of the number seven in the Bible means "completion," Jesus was really saying to Peter that Peter was to forgive "always," and then forgive a vast number of times more than that! How often? Always! Sometimes it takes that many times for our forgiveness to truly be able to be a forgiveness that is "heart felt."

Jesus in Matthew 11 also tells us, "... learn from me..." (Matt 11:29) We do not learn such an important, and oftentimes difficult to grasp and accomplish, lesson overnight and receive a forgiving heart in an instant. It takes a lifetime of continual acts of forgiveness learned from Him who is Mercy Himself. If we want to receive the "tsunami" of Jesus' mercy that He is so very eager to give us, then we must also give mercy to others.

That night after watching the movie and the news with my family, I learned from the encounter with my father that forgiveness is truly given as gift. It is not earned or deserved. I also learned that something small and seemingly lacking in substance, like a feather, has true power and will overcome the forces of unforgiveness when wielded by the hands of God, "for God is Love." (1 John 4:8, 16)

Please absorb this other important takeaway from this event from my life – it is important to realize that God is continually active in the most ordinary day-to-day events of family life. We only need to allow ourselves to be surprised by Him who holds the whole world, the entire universe, in His hands. This includes you.

Yes – you! Now we come to part about "THE Father," your Father and my Father. In the story of our lives that He has written, He has allowed everything in our lives which will lead us to Him. Perhaps you can sense a "desire," often silent, but which is there because it has been placed there by your true Parent, God the Father.

Know it is there – whether silent to you or not. This desire, this place, is there. Our spirit touches this place when we are moved beyond words. We touch it when we think, "If it could only be that way" for us. We touch that place when we experience unconditional love and unconditional forgiveness.

For example, I was giving a retreat for women, when one of them came to see me. This woman had chosen to have nine abortions. As she entered the room to speak to me, she stated, "I am a murderer." She made no excuses. She blamed no one else. She was direct and to the point. When we finished talking, she could only weep without stopping in my arms. On a retreat in Santa Marta, Colombia, I encountered another woman – who, as she knelt with her husband before our Eucharistic Lord, was visited by the Father through Jesus in the monstrance. As she fell to the floor, she said to me, "Father it is beautiful to be loved."

Yes, it is beautiful to be loved. We are transformed when we know we are loved and lovable. However, before I attempt to describe my first encounter with the Father, I will discuss a great obstacle, placed by the Enemy, which is allowed by God so we will know the tactics of the father of lies, Satan. In Revelation 12:10, we are told that Satan is "the accuser." The Enemy accuses us because he does not need to "knock us out" with a mortal sin to separate us from God. Instead, the Enemy often tries to get us to focus on our past sins, even if we have repented of the sins and have been forgiven by God.

The Accuser points out and belabors our past sins, keeping them before us, to stir up a storm, a blinding storm, in our souls. As a result, we lose sight of God in the middle of this spiritual blizzard. It once again is more about "me" and "my sins" than about "me and God." If we lose our peace by focusing on what we did (even though we were already forgiven by God), we allow the father of lies to paint a false image of reality by presenting a half-truth (that what we know we did) as the whole truth.

But knowing and acknowledging that we sinned – that is NOT the whole truth. The Truth is we ARE forgiven, and all is forgotten by Him after His forgiveness of us! So why is this tactic of the Accuser's so common? Because it works all too often. Because it agitates a soul and one is blinded by the lie.

Imagine a lake that has a beautiful mountain peak behind it. If the waters are agitated by wind, the reflection of the mountain in the lake is not clear and is out of focus. So too, if the soul is stirred up and agitated by the father of lies, the soul loses clarity of the absolute goodness and mercy of God. We fail to experience the merciful Father telling us,

"Quickly bring the finest robe and put it on him; put a ring on his finger and sandals on his feet. Take the fatted calf and slaughter it. Then let us celebrate with a feast, because this son of mine was dead, and has come to life again; he was lost, and has been found." (Luke 15:22-24)

Only in peace that comes from facing the truth of our sins and knowing His forgiveness can we "see" the merciful face of God, as He twirls us around in a happy dance because we have returned to Him. He laughs with joy, a joy that cannot fully be put into human words. Have you ever heard the Father laugh with joy as He twirls you around and says, "You're home. You are home. You are finally home."?

A priest I know describes the experience he lived within his soul while giving a retreat. This priest loves the Church and loves being a priest. He shares, "A woman who had not been to confession in over 30 years came to me and asked me to hear her confession…As I had finished hearing her confession and had given her words of encouragement and a few Scriptures to meditate on, I began to pray the words of absolution. When I gave her absolution, I suddenly experienced within myself the love and presence of God the Father looking at her. I did not cause this nor could I stop it.

"The love I experienced almost killed me! When I finished saying the prayer of absolution, out of my mouth came laughter and a celebration. She could only cry and cry, and I could only laugh for joy that she was finally home." This priest's story shows us how he felt the Father in him celebrating the return of His daughter. And she later spoke at the end of the retreat that she experienced the Father's welcome and celebration of her homecoming.

Paul tells us in Galatians 2:20, "... yet I live, no longer I, but Christ lives in me..." And since Jesus and the Father are One (John 10:30), to see and experience Jesus is to see and experience the Father! This priest, acting in the person of Christ in confession, experienced the Father looking at this daughter His coming home. My priest friend would later say, "The love and joy I experienced was not of this world! I felt so much love that I felt I was going to literally die of love." And the woman, she "tasted" the joy and laughter of the Father through the priest. Most people I have talked to have not experienced such a tangible encounter with the Father in the sacrament of confession. This is a great grace, and a gift that God knew she needed.

The joy and celebration in the heart of the Father is every bit as great as this priest and woman experienced. In my travels to many countries giving retreats, I hear of many testimonies of people having deep, tangible encounters with God or the saints while on retreat or at Mass. I wonder if the Father, through such encounters, is crying out to the world that has become deafened by sin. I am less and less surprised to hear of such events. I humbly believe there is a real urgency at this time in history, with heaven calling out to us, crying out to us, "Come home!"

I will end this reflection on forgiveness with a true story. An amazing 81-year-old Jesuit priest, named Father Ignacio Muggido, shared with my community a wonderful story that he experienced when he was a novice. After the Spanish Civil War, he and other Jesuits would visit town by town in Spain to have days of reconciliation with town locals. During the war, caused by a deep split in Spain between those who supported General Francisco Franco and those who opposed him, many died and a great many were martyred for the Faith.

Once during the last evening of one of these retreats on forgiveness, this Jesuit priest witnessed an encounter involving a man whose son had been murdered by a neighbor of theirs during the civil war. As the end of the gathering approached, the priest at the town square shouted, "Before we leave this town, is there anyone else that needs to be forgiven or has to ask forgiveness?" A man came forward and said that he needed to forgive the man in front of him, the neighbor who murdered his son. The murdered son's father approached the neighbor man guilty of murder. Then this still-mourning father opened his arms to embrace the murderer. As he told his son's killer "I forgive you," he died in the arms of that murderer. To forgive the man who murdered his son cost this father everything, including his very life.

I realize to call God "Father" is for many very painful to even hear. I have heard of a woman telling a priest on a retreat, "Please call God anything, but do not call him "Father." So, I share with you a taste of what Pope Benedict XVI says in his wonderful book, *Jesus of Nazareth*, that "the gift of God is God Himself." [44]

The Father is not just interested to meet our needs but to MEET us – by giving Himself to you and to me. So let us let Him Father us and surprise us. Again, quoting Pope Benedict XVI, "To name God as Father thus becomes a summons to us; to live as a 'child,' as a son or daughter. 'All that is mine is thine,' Jesus says in his high-priestly prayer to the Father (John 17:10), and the father says the same thing to the elder brother of the Prodigal Son in the story (Luke 15:31). The word father is an invitation to live from our awareness of this reality." [45]

I invite you and recommend that you to take this invitation to heart and answer the summons of which the late Pope

---

[44] Ratzinger, Joseph. *Jesus of Nazareth*, Page 136.
[45] Ibid. Page 138.

Benedict wrote, and that we know that all of which is of the Father is ours. A living, dynamic relationship with the Father as a son or a daughter in the Son, Jesus, can be ours. Let us expect and work for nothing less. Let us say, "Yes" to this invitation to live, as much as is possible on this side of eternity, the life of a son or a daughter of the Father.

So, walk along with me as I describe some encounters during my life with the Father, my Papa. In the following prayer, I attempt to describe in a nutshell what it felt like for me to be "seen" by Papa for the first time:

> "O Papa, I have met your eternal gaze.
> I asked you to look at me
> And You did.
> O Papa to be 'seen' by You is to be seen by heaven.
> Your eyes calmed my fears.
> Your eyes quieted my sense of worthlessness.
> Your eyes lifted me from myself to Yourself.
> I knew I was created to live on "earth as it is in heaven"
> Under Your loving gaze.
> So, I tell You over and over again, 'Look at me!'
> In Your gaze I discover I am Yours and You are mine.
> Your gaze lifts me; gives me courage; quiets my fears.
> It recreates me and shows me who I am – Your son!
> When I 'see' You looking at me, I know I am Home,

For You are my home!"

I came to call the Father "Papa" because this is what sprang up in the deepest part of my being during this first experience of feeling and tasting His loving gaze upon me as a son. His son! This initial experience of Papa's "noticing" me occurred during my personal and silent priest retreat in 1998. I was in New Hampshire with a wonderful woman, who was giving me a retreat about *True Devotion to Mary* by St. Louis-Marie de Montfort. While in prayer before Jesus in the Blessed Sacrament, suddenly I saw a large "being," a "man" from the vantage point of my soul. I saw no face, but I knew it was not Jesus.

It was my Papa. When I "saw" Him during my meditation, I sensed Him say to me, "When I see you, I see my Son." I almost lost it. I was seen not as "Philip," but as Jesus. I was sent into the most exquisite fire, a passion of love, and was enveloped by a "fire" that I had never known. As Papa "looked" at me, I was no longer aware of myself. Rather, it was truly He, the Father, looking at me with the gaze, the passion, of a Father towards His son. I knew I was a "son" in the Son, Jesus. There was a place for me, an eternal place, in the Father's heart. How long this "seeing" lasted I do not know. The all-important thing was that I was home, in my Papa's Heart.

Do you understand? We were meant to be noticed – and to be known. In Scripture we are told, "Before I formed you in the womb I knew you..." (Jer 1:5) This "being known" is a "belonging" to Him. We are His. And He is ours, "our Father." Oh, we have "*things*," but they do not and cannot "know" us and we do not know them. We have a place, a home, but we do not belong there. We live there, but we are not there as we are in the Father. In the Father, you are known with a Love that goes all the way down into the smallest part of yourself. This gives us a place where we truly and fully belong and can be for all eternity.

We have never left His knowing. We have never been any place else. This place is "from ever" to "forever." It was "before," and it is an eternal "now." It is forever! The experience of being "known" by Him draws us to Him, and we are never, and we will never be, far from His loving gaze.

Addressing the Athenians, St. Paul says, "For 'In Him we live, and move, and have our being.'"(Acts 17:28) This "being seen" by Him gives us a sense and a confidence that we really are His, and only His. Our belonging to someone here on earth is temporary, and just for the moment. Yet both on earth and in eternity, we are never out of His sight and always belong to Him. We can feel and we can trust what Dorothy in the movie "The Wizard of Oz" said, "There is no place like home."

This is truly the Truth that has been written throughout salvation history, and that we can continue to write as we live our lives in the now – our true home is the heart of the Father. All of us, with every bit of ourselves, ought to naturally desire to be exposed to the loving gaze of the Father. During my first personal encounter with my Papa, I experienced a gaze that is beautifully described in the book of Sirach as "the eyes of the LORD [are] ten thousand times brighter than the sun..." (Sir 23:19) And these Eternal Eyes which are "ten thousand times brighter than the sun" dry every tear and heal every wound under their gaze.

This is why I found the Fatherhood of my Papa to be more real, more the Truth, than my "father wound" had been. For me, the words Psalm 27:10 (ESV) began to become truly my reality, "For my father and mother have forsaken me, but the LORD will take me in."

All was truly gift.

And you, who are reading these words, I ask you, has the gaze of the Father touched you? Let us pray,

> O Father, You know I have a deep longing to be noticed. I have sought 'eyes' that would notice me in the wrong places and wrong ways. Today I realize that it was Your Eyes I desired to notice me.

I ask you, "Look at me!" I know You are near. I need to know your love! Thank you for allowing me to be "seen" by You, my Father!" [46]

I could never "see" You by my own effort. Only when first You "saw" could I "see." I felt like a little boy whose legs could not touch the floor, like one whose Father had to "lift me up and out of myself," out of my "father wound," by fixing Your eternal gaze upon me. My reality became You, and I did not even remember "me." I only saw and knew You. Amen.

The way someone sees you can transform you. That is so true. If you are seen with dislike, it will affect you. If you are seen with love, you are changed. Now, imagine being "seen" by LOVE itself, God. You know you have an identity that is not merely the summation of your choices. It is not even the totality of others' opinions of you.

There is but one opinion that must count – one perspective that must silence, must quiet the opinions of others, including those of our parents and our own; opinions that often come from our limited perspective bound by time and space. We are told by St. Paul in 1 Corinthians 13:12

---

[46] "What eye has not seen, and ear has not heard, and what has not entered the human heart, what God has prepared for those who love him." (1 Cor 2:9)

> "At present we see indistinctly, as in a mirror, but then face to face. At present I know partially; then I shall know fully, as I am fully known."

However, the Father's perspective of you is clear from his all-seeing and omniscient point of view, and His perspective is what it always has been since He first even just thought of creating you. The Father's perspective of you just IS…period. It does not change.

I remember at first trying to recall my sins, my years of rebellion against Him. I tried to convince Him of my serious sinfulness by saying, "But, but...what about "this?" What about "that?" The sinfulness did not matter to Him any longer. It was lost and drowned by the merciful Precious Blood of Jesus. Are there past sins that still drown out the loving gaze of God in your life? Is who you are more about your past sins than of His eternal perspective of you?

We are reminded in Psalm 103:12, 14 that

> "as far as the east is from the west, so far has he removed our sins from us… For he knows how we are formed, remembers that we are dust."

If our focus is not Him, we do not "see" well at all…rather like the reflection of the mountain peak on the disturbed surface of the lake at the mountain's foot, as mentioned earlier in this chapter. Be consoled that even though He knows all about us, including our sins and any shame, we are and will remain, when all is said and done – only His. He will not abandon us.

You are the only you.

A good parent explains to his son or daughter the mysteries of the child's life and the movements of the children's hearts. God does not do any less, and this is how my Good Parent, my Papa, explained one of my life's mysteries to me...

I always had a clouded heart because I didn't like my name. I looked forward to changing my name when I began my community, but as I thought about it, I thought I would cause confusion in the Catholic world because I was already established in my name, Father Philip Scott. Yet, I always had a slight envy of my community's members who were able to choose their own religious names when they received their religious habits. I felt left out.

God knew this and He addressed it with me during the closing Mass of a retreat. As I was purifying the chalice at the end of the communion rite, I experienced His Presence around me and I heard His voice say to me "I know you've never liked your name." I began to cry. Those attending the retreat must have wondered, "Why is he crying? He has purified the chalice many times." I nodded to Him to communicate that "Yes, I've never liked my name." Those in the pews must have wondered why I was nodding now. However, I was lost in the Father and barely aware of the congregation.

It was Him and me alone in the church. He went on to ask me, "Do you know why you are named Philip?" I shook my head "no." Then He asked me, "What did the apostle Philip ask my son?" The apostle Philip said, "Show us the Father and that will be enough for us." (John 14:8) Then my Father said this to me, "Is this not a perpetual longing in your heart?" I nodded, "Yes." Then He said, "And so your longing will be fulfilled!"

It was then I realized that my very name connects me with my perpetual and my deepest desire to see the Father, who is my Papa. My name is an echo of my longing for the Father! I could not begin to make this experience up!

When I experienced my Papa's presence, I felt I was truly the only "Philip" that existed before Him. I know there are many, many Philips in our world and throughout the history of humanity. The point is this – God loves you and me as if we each were the only one for Him. A rabbi of the Middle Ages translated the words describing His Name as given to Moses in Exodus 3:14, "I Am Who Am" to "I am here for you."

In every tabernacle in every Catholic Church in the world, He whispers, "I am here for you." As if you were the only person created. Something wonderful and amazing happens when you realize that ALL of God is there, and is "here" now for you. Every movement of your life is a place for Him. In your sadness – He is there for you. In your joy – He is there for you. In your failures and in your sin – He is there for you. In such places and at such moments where He and I have been together, I just tell Him, "Papa, look at me."

A beautiful verse in the Bible describes this invitation from Him to allow Him to be "more" real than what we feel or experience at each moment. We read in Psalm 46:11, "Be still and know that I am God!" This type of "knowing" – that God directs all things, people, time – means experiencing that He has the last word; that He is God! God knows you like no other, even to the point in Scripture that describes Him as having the hairs of our head counted.

During one of my private retreats, I sat in prayer in silence. I do not know if you have ever heard the Father's voice. It is different from the voice of Jesus. His voice inspires a realization that He has an authority which keeps the universe intact. As I continued in silent prayer, I seemed to hear the words, "Once upon a time...Once upon a time...Once upon a time..." As I heard the beginning of what sounded like a story begging to be told to me, I was engulfed in sense of "I am here now, for you. And I have always been here for you!"

The Voice came again. "Once upon a time there was a Philip, my only Philip..." It was Him, my Papa telling me a story, my story, as seen from His perspective. I dissolved completely when I heard, "My only Philip..." I felt I was the only one He ever knew and saw and understood. And I wept and wept. The warm paternity of His Voice filled me, protected me, sheltered me, was for me, and spoke that He was in my corner. It made me know and experience I was His and He was mine. He went on to share His Heart with me as He allowed me to feel in my own heart His pain for having sent me into a family where little love existed.

My heart felt like it was going to burst because of pain just to experience His pain. I literally felt like I was going to die. I cried and cried. Then I heard in my heart, "But it was necessary for Me to do this." He allowed me to be born into a family where there was little love, because of the mission He had set for me, the mission to heal the family. I realized He saw me not just from heaven's perspective but from within me. He really knew (far more than I did) my pain while growing up at home. His Heart, His pain was the "real thing." It was more real than me alone with just my pain and my experience during those years at home.

He showed me a memory that no one other than me knew. I saw myself around the age of nine with my first dog, a beagle named Pluto. Pluto and I went everywhere together. During the winter months I would cuddle him next to me and we would hide underneath the bathroom sink next to the vent where the heat would come out. Eventually we would both fall asleep. No one knew this was my and Pluto's special hiding place. In my nine-year-old mind, I felt Pluto understood and loved me, as I too understood and loved him.

On October 9, 1970, my Pluto was hit by a car. Pluto dragged himself to our house, where we found him with tire marks on his broken body. We took him to the animal hospital and they operated but nothing could be done. Pluto's pelvis had been smashed. The next morning the veterinarian called to tell us that he did all he could, but that they had to put him to sleep. I answered the phone when the veterinarian called. Dropping the phone, I began to run and kept shouting and crying aloud, "No, No!"

because I knew Pluto was no longer living. My beloved dog was gone from my life, and my world fell apart. That same weekend my sister got married, and my grandmother died.

From my nine-year old perspective, the death of Pluto was more painful than my grandmother's death. God the Father knew this. Papa knew EVERYTHING. Each memory was not just shown to me. Rather, I experienced His Heart seeing me and felt His pains at my sufferings. As I experienced the loss of Pluto, I was even shown how for weeks I would go to "our place" where we would cuddle and I would look for any of Pluto's hairs and scratch marks left by his paws when he would see other dogs in the park across from our house. These details were not unnoticed by my Papa. He saw and felt every bit of pain and joy that I experienced during Pluto's short life with me. I came to understand why I clung so much to Pluto as I had not clung to my parents. I truly experienced, during this retreat at the age of 49, that every tear of mine was important to my Papa.

During each memory Papa showed me, I literally felt as if I was being rocked back and forth in a rocking chair in my Papa's Heart. As each new memory showing began, I would once again hear the words, "Once upon a time..." I tell you that I experienced being KNOWN as no one else had ever been known. Yet as I am on the outside of this experience now, I realize that is not true. He knows all His sons and daughters perfectly. But to be SEEN in such detail was to be known as no other person. I know there are events in our lives more serious than the death of our dog or cat. But I believe, from the Father's perspective, everything…everything is important to Him.

NO detail of your life or mine goes unnoticed by the Father. For years I had lived with these memories as if they really were no big deal. But all of them matter to my Papa. For Him, the very sound of my voice, my tears moved Him beyond and more than my heart's capacity to feel and experience His Heart. I was overwhelmed, to the point of being brought to the point of feeling I would be crushed by the intensity of His pain at my suffering. For me, the memory was long past. For my Father, it was ever before Him. The experience lasted for hours.

Yet I too know that when I cried over the Pluto's death, it was for moments that occurred at points in time. Yet, in eternity, there are no moments, no time as we know it, and what becomes more real is the Father and not the events or moments. Every experience seen from His perspective draws us to the powerful influence of His Fatherhood and away from our limited viewpoints. The Father's perspective becomes more real than the experience that we remember.

His being with you in moments of your suffering and pain needs to impact and touch you and me more than the force of the event. Here Heaven's perspective improves our vision, the vision distorted by suffering and sin – ours and others sins that wounded us. Why is this so? Our life events pass and yet God never passes. He never "was" or "will be" anywhere than where He is in His eternal now. He is always with you…always with me. What this soul experience taught me at a deep, heart level is that God ALONE is enough!

In 2 Corinthians 12:9, St. Paul was told this by our Lord when he heard, "My grace is sufficient for you…" Grace is not a "something." Grace is God, His very life. He was trying to "seal" into me that "I (God) Am sufficient for you." It takes a lifetime to plumb the depths of this Truth. We will not be able (or allowed) to enter our real home of heaven until we really "live, move, and have our being" in this – God ALONE SUFFICES!!

During the part of Mass called the penitential rite, I often am brought back interiorly to being rocked back and forth in my Papa's Heart. While the congregation and I pray "Lord, have mercy… Christ, have mercy…Lord, have mercy," I am being held in His arms like a child being rocked back and forth as I admit my sinfulness. For me, this is being at HOME. Later in the Mass, within the context of the eucharistic celebration and in prayer before

Jesus in the Blessed Sacrament, I experience being a little boy. In my heart I see myself being rocked back and forth. In this scene, I am so little that my feet cannot touch the ground. But that does not matter, because I want to stay there. I know He wants me to experience this and to return there when trials come and go.

To meet the Father is to be the undivided object of His attention. In this earthly life, it is demeaning to be someone's object. One feels used. But to be the object of the Father's love is to be healed and lifted beyond who I think I am – to be lifted up before the Father. And in such moments, I am known by Him like no one else. He knows all creatures and creation with the same level of infinite detail and knowledge. But for me, in my deepest part of who I am, He treats me like I am the only one for Him.

Truly how one is seen can change you. How else can I describe this? Imagine a light that is 10,000 times stronger than the sun facing you. The whole of your being is touched in such a way that words fall far short of your joy and gratitude.

What love! What a Papa!

Chapter Ten – Who You Really Are – A Life of Being Forgiven

"Not only do we know God by Jesus Christ alone, but we know ourselves only by Jesus Christ. We know life and death only through Jesus Christ. Apart from Jesus Christ, we do not know what is our life, nor our death, nor God, nor ourselves."

— Blaise Pascal

St. John of the Cross once said, "The soul in its darkness groans under its chains, motionless, helpless, until the spirit is softened, humbled, purified, made so subtle, so simple, that it can, in some way, become one with the spirit of God, in accordance with the extent and degree of the union of love to which mercy wishes to raise it."

God has from all eternity planned for each individual soul to live in union with Him and reach a depth or level of perfection and holiness to most glorify Him. This cannot occur without suffering. John of Avila once said, "Christ tells us if we want to join him, we shall travel the way he took. It is surely not right that the Son of God should go this way on the path of shame while the sons of men walk the way of worldly honor."

Remember hearing the words, "No pain, no gain?" The way to heaven is NOT one that is without pain – it is not a cake walk; it is not without tears. One does not grow to become a beautiful rose in God's garden without encountering thorns. We have looked at the suffering one feels in moments when we are shown our poverty, our sin. These moments are painful because of our pride. We are surprised because we do not see ourselves as we really are, but rather as we think we are or as others see us. We need God's perspective – His Truth, which requires humility.

So, let us change our perspective in order to make more sense (for us) about how suffering is a vital part of the life of a son or daughter of the Father. If we are to be included among those to whom Jesus told such words as, "But blessed are your eyes, because they see, and your ears, because they hear." (Matt 13:16), we must accept that there is no growth without suffering. We do not see Him better or hear His voice more clearly without suffering.

We have, in Jesus, the supreme model of One Who Suffered. Upon seeing the risen Lord in heaven, John wrote, "Then I saw standing in the midst of the throne and the four living creatures and the elders, a Lamb that seemed to have been slain."(Rev 5:6) As Venerable Bishop Fulton Sheen used to say, "Jesus is not "Jesus Christ – Super Star, but "Jesus Christ – Super Scar." We are most Christ-like when in some way we share in His "scars" – that is, in His suffering.

At first, our moments and events accompanied by suffering make God's voice that would comfort seem so distant that it seems unhearable, perhaps even altogether silent. Why is this so? We do not understand love – real love. The world speaks of a love without suffering, one filled with only pleasure. Since life is to be a school that teaches us to love we must look at the real thing – Love, which is of heaven. It is of another universe. Love is not "made in the USA" like Ford cars and trucks.

We are born spiritually deaf and blind, in fact spiritually "stillborn." Think about this – we were born spiritually dead! So, God must raise us to life, and I do not mean a natural life where only the body functions. For this rising to life in God, we must allow Him to make our being subject to the Holy Spirit, for those who are led by the Spirit are sons and daughters of God.

As we work on being subject to the Holy Spirit, we also come to a more truthful sense of reality – and that the "real thing" is not Coca-Cola™, but Jesus. And that Jesus is Love – the divine "insanity" of Love made flesh. It is important to remember that only what is Christ-like can pass Go on the Monopoly™ game that is our earthly life into eternal life – and that is something Jesus already won for us.

Why does this have to be? Little by little we realize that without the grace, the breath of God, we are like the dead bones described in Ezekiel 37:1-11. Parents in infant baptism are asked, "What do you ask for...?" They answer "Baptism." It is through baptism that we begin to receive not "human" help, but God's help. We are brought to life spiritually. St. Paul wrote, "…are you unaware that we who were baptized into Christ Jesus were baptized into his death? We were indeed buried with him through baptism into death, so that, just as Christ was raised from the dead by the glory of the Father, we too might live in newness of life." (Rom 6:3-4)

This newness of life is not meant to lead me to live life just as Philip Scott, but like Christ. Why is this? St. Paul wrote about us in his letter to the Romans.

> "For those he foreknew he also predestined to be conformed to the image of his Son, so that he might be the firstborn among many brothers. And those he predestined he also called; and those he called he also justified; and those whom he justified he also glorified."
> (Rom 8:29-30)

Jesus is our Divine Elder Brother and we are among the "many brothers." Though He alone is the Son, we are adopted as sons and daughters through baptism. He is the Way, though "How narrow the gate and constricted the road that leads to life. And those who find it are few." (Matt 7:14)

Those sons and daughters that follow His Way, and use the narrow gate, will also be glorified with Jesus and share in His glory. This sharing is not automatic but is conditional. St. Paul sheds light on how a son or daughter shares the glory of Jesus when he writes in his letter to the Romans "... if only we suffer with him so that we may also be glorified with him" (Rom 8:17).

This suffering comes in many ways. It can come in the form of temptations as seen in the life of Jesus (Matt 4:1-11). Or the suffering may come in the form of rejection from the world, as He too was rejected. Remember Our Lord said,

> "If the world hates you, realize that it hated me first. If you belonged to the world, the world would love its own; but because you do not belong to the world, and I have chosen you out of the world, the world hates you. Remember the word I spoke to you, 'No slave is greater than his master.' If they persecuted me, they will also persecute you..." (John 15:18-20).

Or the suffering may come from sorrow that comes from seeing our sin (known as contrition), as in "Blessed are they who mourn, for they will be comforted." (Matt 5:4) This suffering, when united to Christ's suffering, does not kill, but gives you life, and gives it abundantly. It becomes a means to "do" a work in us. It can remove the most stubborn stains of sin from our souls as St. Peter writes in his first letter,

> "Therefore, since Christ suffered in the flesh, arm yourselves also with the same attitude (for whoever suffers in the flesh has broken with sin)." (1 Pet 4:1)

Suffering can be used by God in such a way as to free us from the grip of sin on our lives. When people suffer, their eyes, their focus, can be raised to God and away from themselves. One can see the consequences of sin, and begin to hate sin and see sin for what it really is. We see it is not in any way good or sweet. Suffering brings about DEEP cleaning and healing – getting all the way down to the "roots" of our sins. When united to Christ, our suffering is truly healing, for "…by His stripes we were healed." (Isa 53:5)

In whatever way God allows one of His children to suffer, if the suffering is united to the cross of Jesus, it is of great profit. St. Peter writes,

> "... although now for a little while you may have to suffer through various trials, so that the genuineness of your faith, more precious than gold that is perishable even though tested by fire, may prove to be for praise, glory, and honor at the revelation of Jesus Christ. Although you have not seen him you love him; even though you do not see him now yet believe in him, you rejoice with an indescribable and glorious joy, as you attain the goal of (your) faith, the salvation of your souls."
> (1 Pet 1:6-9)

Suffering cuts through any part of our "identity" that is not yet like Jesus, Who is our true identity. Suffering cuts away our false self. When we die, we will present to Jesus our true face and all our masks will be stripped away. This true face is one we draw ourselves, slowly and exercising our free will in making one choice after another. St. Augustine once said, "He who created us without us will not save us without us."

So, we must co-operate with His grace, responding to Him "Yes," and giving Him our fiat – allowing Jesus to live and be formed in us. It is our "yes" to Him that makes it possible for Paul's words that ring true, "…work out your salvation with fear and trembling."(Phil 2:12) This "working out our salvation" is an all-consuming, sometimes even tedious, process.

It is not for the faint of heart.

Only what is wholly "Christ-like" (spotless, without blemish, as was required of the sacrificial lambs required for that first Passover) is allowed to enter heaven and spend eternity in the presence of the Beatific Vision. Whoever is not yet entirely Christ-like at the time of death must be purified in purgatorial fire
> "For our God is a consuming fire." (Heb 12:29), and because

> "nothing unclean will enter [heaven]…" (Rev 21:27)

Part of the suffering we experience occurs when we are not faithful to God and instead commit sin. In Psalm 51 we read,

> "Against you, you alone have I sinned; I have done what is evil in your eyes…My Sacrifice, O God, is a contrite spirit; a contrite, humbled heart, O God you will not scorn." (Ps. 51:6, 19)

Being cleansed of a sinful, sin-filled spirit is agonizing; yet if we are contrite and humble ourselves before the just hand of God, He will lift us up. This self-response to our suffering raises our eyes toward God. It is not a "poor pitiful me" attitude where we beat ourselves with a "wet noodle." It is truly a mourning or a crying out that is pleasing to God's eyes and ears.

Why? Because Jesus too

> "offered prayers and supplications with loud cries and tears to the one who was able to save him from death, and he was heard because of his reverence." (Heb. 5:7)

So, when we cry out from the depths of our being, we share in Jesus' tears and have hope that our cries too will be heard by our Father.

Once I was on my priest retreat and on my arrival to the retreat house, as I sat down to eat dinner, I had a deep desire to cry. This surprised me because my retreat was just beginning. My heart knew what my head did not. As I wondered what was going on, I just said, "Yes," giving my fiat to whatever the Spirit was doing in me. It was not long before I began to see what was being done in me and for me. It was a special grace.

What was this grace, this gift? We read in Matthew 5, "Blessed are they who mourn, for they will be comforted." (Matt 5:4) What I am about to discuss might seem to some as an exaggeration, a holy hyperbole. To those who believe God is love (and He is, 1 John 4:16) but who also live a **false** belief that His Love is blind, and that He looks at our sinfulness and says, "No big deal," – you might be tempted to skip this section of the book.

Please resist this temptation.

For that is what it is – a temptation from the father of all lies, Satan himself. And your Enemy's goal is to keep you away from the Father of Truth who most assuredly loves us as we are, but Who (even more) loves you and me far too much to let us remain that way. So, bear with me. Realize there is no way to exaggerate this experience.

As the retreat began, I was being shown little by little my past sins. Little by little, I increasingly felt crushed by them, and the weight of my sinfulness was unbearable. During each hour I spent in prayer before Jesus in the Blessed Sacrament, it was as if I was being shown a spiritual movie of my sinfulness as God saw it.

For instance, in my youth I saw my "partying" as fun, but now I saw – really saw – the lie of that youthful lifestyle, that it in truth was a sharing in the culture of death. I remembered that I once thought to myself, "Boy, this is life" only to realize later this so-called life was, in reality, nothing but death and a living hell. What I had valued as "life" and fun," was neither one of those things, but was truthfully a slow dying, for it was a life of chronic mortal sin.

Saint Paul tells us that those who do such things will not inherit the kingdom of God. These sins are what Paul calls the works of the flesh, and that to do such works and not repent is to die a spiritual death – to lose the presence of God in the soul. In addition to their prophesied physical deaths, this death of the Spirit in their souls was experienced by Adam and Eve when they disobeyed God in the Garden of Eden.

I saw my spiritual state in all its shameful truth before my Father. This experience had me focus on the truth and light of the Father as never before in my life, with my attention turned towards the Father and away from myself. Nor was I able to think interiorly even "poor me," because I was in such a wretched state. All I could do was cry out to the Father, "Father, have mercy on me, as I have so offended You."

I repeat, the focus was not on me but on God. It was an exquisite but painful experience, but I knew this "seeing" and true acknowledgement of my sinfulness, from God's perspective, was absolutely necessary and just. I knew I deserved hell and eternal separation from His goodness, and realized that only because of His mercy could I be saved from hell. All I could do for that week was cry for the many ways I had offended Jesus, Who is Love, by my sinfulness.

How much time, how much of my life, I wastefully spent on a way of life that was not the life of a "son" of the Light, of the "adopted son of God" He intended me to be! For that week, I saw my life through the lens of God's justice, and was crushed by the weight of my sinfulness. The priest who was directing me on this retreat reminded me that

God was allowing me to "taste and see" His justice. God's justice was one side of the coin.

My priest retreat leader also told me that I was being shown where I stood. If only God's justice was considered, I deserved hell. Believe me this is not some overly scrupulous exaggeration, and truly is a fact, and not born out of low self-esteem. It is the truth and nothing but the truth. I stood before the infinite love of God, Truth itself and knew I deserved eternal separation from Him.

There was no way to dodge this bullet, and nowhere I could hide from Him. His bullet of Love hit me square in my heart.

During this retreat, as I awakened to the truths the Father was showing me, I found I could not distance myself from the experience, this act of a loving Father. There was nowhere to run or hide from Him and the Truth. These words of Psalm 139 were a bedrock of my living reality,

> "Where can I go from your spirit? From your presence, where can I flee?" (Psalm 139:7)

I only knew that my future would end with an eternity in hell, were it not for His total mercy.

There are times one is blessed with a clearer perspective, more than only a mere concept of an eternal truth. Here one is shown what is not possible to see with our human, non-spiritually aided eyes. According to the verdict before the throne of God's justice, I was guilty due to my past choices. But I am forgiven and saved by God's choice to love me and forgive me, even though it cost Him death, death on the cross. O blessed Cross!

That God allows us to share in this cross is a gift and a blessing. For we are saved by God's mercy, freely given to us through Christ's willing sacrificial death on the cross. That sounds nice and clear, right? Well, I **thought** I "got it" and understood that truth in the seminary and in my apologetics discussions with fellow Christians who are not Catholic. But I really did not get it.

I certainly had not truly experienced this gift of mercy, until the Father opened it for me during this retreat. This opening of God's gift of mercy was not a small matter, nor was it painless.

The human spirit is able to "know" in a way and at a depth that our mind cannot. Realizing the true state of my soul crushed me, and I saw myself standing empty before God. The experience was utterly terrifying at best. My tears came from the depths of my being, and I knew now that I was a walking blob of sin. I walked the path of what

Scripture speaks of when it says, "Deep calls to deep…." (Ps 42:8) I called from the depth of my sinful state to His mercy, a mercy which I could not see or feel anywhere.

I found myself trudging heavily through my misery, my felt inability to be pleasing to God. This was the most terrifying retreat of my life!

Let me state it again. The facts were clear and uncontestable – I was guilty and deserved eternal damnation. I looked desperately for anything that I could hang on to that would save me. I found nothing.

No cry of mine was ever loud enough to reach the ears of the Father and soften His justice. My voice was not the voice that could or would hold back the justice of God I deserved. Only the Voice of His Son, His only begotten Son, could save me. And I owe all praise, devotion and love to Jesus, who alone was the One who cried out two thousand years ago "Father, forgive him, your Philip." I knew it was all Gift, a gift that cost my Papa's Son His life.

This Truth, and the role my own sinfulness and that of the rest of humankind played in bringing it about, is painful to receive. It strips us of any sense of believing "I am not that bad." Yes, we have been that bad, we are that bad, and we may well be again in the future.

This is not a simplistic expression of self-hatred. On the contrary. Understanding and acknowledging the role that our sinfulness plays in our lives, and that it was the reason for Jesus' sacrifice on the cross, is a healthy truth that sets us free.

It is a truth that heals me, and heals each of us, but still feels like it is wounding us. That is what suffering does when it is accepted and united to Jesus' Cross – it saves us from ourselves. It raises our eyes to God and to heaven. At first, suffering blinds us and we cry out, "If God is good, then why does God allow this?"

With time and a silence impregnated by God Himself, we begin to see that if God allows suffering it is because it is necessary and useful for His ends.

We must say, "Thy will be done," and sincerely MEAN it. Over and over again – especially when we suffer! In his book on suffering called *Making Sense Out of Suffering*, Peter Kreeft wrote

> "Here is how fiat, 'thy will be done,' transforms suffering…If I want x and I get y instead, I suffer, both because I do not get x, which I want, and also because I get y, which I do not want. But if I want only God's will, I do not suffer, because I always

get God's will. *Thus, paradoxically, the essence of suffering (death to self-will) can become its opposite (perfect joy) when it is undertaken freely for love of God.* [Emphasis mine.] God not only compensates us for suffering, He turns suffering itself into perfect joy, if only we obey his first and greatest commandment wholeheartedly, if we only love and will and worship him alone and above all." [47]

None of us can do this perfectly. Each time we say "yes" to whatever comes our way through life can prepare us for the next time to say to the Father, "Fiat. Thy will be done." Then we begin to realize when something happens to us, whether we desire it or not, it has the Father's stamp of approval on it. This something is His perfect will or at least His permissive will. It will be for our good somehow, whether seen from our limited perspective while on earth or from heaven's eternal viewpoint.

At times God allows the unthinkable, the never-before imagined event that knocks us "down for the count." Some time ago, my community had been in Peru for a few years and things were going well. We were growing and the charism of the community to heal the family was flowing as we met many families who were reached at every level.

---

[47] Kreeft, Peter. *Making Sense Out of Suffering*. Page 145.

I sensed the Lord say to me on my private retreat, "My son, prepare for a difficult trial that is approaching." I thought to myself, "Maybe I will be kidnapped again and hopefully this time they will finish the job and kill me." (After I was released from the kidnapping and not killed – though I had gotten ever so close – I had been left with a desire for eternity that consumed me.)

Soon after that, our community's Mother Superior, whom I had known and worked alongside for over two decades, came back from her home and family visit. I had been in Los Angeles preaching at an apologetics conference for Hispanics, and my return flight to Peru was late. I called the community to tell them I would arrive at 2:30 a.m., and Mother Superior answered the phone and told me we would catch up. I slept for two hours and went to the sisters' convent for lunch. After lunch she said, "Let's go to get a cup of coffee to catch up."

We sat down and she looked straight at me and said, "I am going home." When I heard those words, I was both shocked and speechless. It was like having your heart hit broad-side by a huge 18-wheeler truck. Sometime before leaving for her home visit, she had written two letters to give to her family in case she was ever martyred. And had also told me from time to time, "Father there is no place I would rather be (in Peru)." She was happy, incredibly happy as a missionary sister in Peru.

Yes, the Mother of our family, our community, had decided to leave. (When I speak to one of a couple who had a spouse walk out on them, this person describes his or her pain in a similar manner.) I cannot and will not analyze Mother Superior's heart and what happened to her during her visit home. What I do want to tell you, who perhaps have had a similar "abandonment" or experience that hit you broadside, is how such unwanted events are used to teach us and form "sonship" in us. And I would like to share with you, my dear friend, how God used this experience to lead me to the Father.

When she left, I was in shock. I cried and was angry. For six months after her departure, I would go to bed, knowing I would sleep little and often be awakened by my emotional pain. I remember seeing my community eat their dessert after what would be the first Thanksgiving meal without her. We ate with a silence that filled the room and our hearts. It was a silence that showed our wounds. My heart broke for them, but I could not take away their pain.

Interiorly, I argued with her in my heart, "I hope you are happy! Was it worth it? Look what you have done to us!" I swallowed tears as I chewed my food.

At first our prayers in such moments are raised, but they seem to fall back to the ground as a deflated balloon quickly falls back to earth after being tossed into the sky. I too was deflated, like that balloon. The pain of her departure remained in the forefront of my heart, and God was nowhere to be found.

I lived in this state for some time! The suffering I experienced in my soul was longer than the suffering that had been caused by any human event. Rather, my suffering resulted from a touch by the "finger of God," and which in turn led to a "dark night of the soul," as my spiritual director called it. This touch from God's finger was a passive kind, but I realized that I had not initiated it, nor could I bring it to an end. I say "passive" for a person is the passive recipient of God's purifying action. The suffering will last as long as God finds it necessary and according to His plans for a person's life.

Three years passed, during which time I lived in this "dark night" state of interior pain. In any case, it was now October 21, 2008, and I made a long entry in my journal describing my soul's state. The entry is long, but I believe it is well worth reading and hope it will be helpful to you.

> "...I am tired of the interior pain. I spoke with "Y," and she described to me the state of my soul – What I am living. She told me I would not be able to make

'heads or tails' of what she was telling me when we ended the telephone conversation. It was true. What I am living is You, my Everything – but You come to me without a face and with Your cross that crushes me. What pain! I feel a loneliness – a separation. I do not feel a part of You, a part of the community that I have founded; I feel totally alone. I belong to nothing and to nobody. I only feel at "home" in my pain – in my darkness, in my rejection. It is so clear; I belong to nobody. I repeat often that I belong to You. I am Yours. But I feel and experience a total sense of rejection, pain, and out of place – to a point that even in my own being I do not belong.

"Whose am I? I hope I belong to You. Only to You, my Jesus. But I also feel in me my reality of a cold wall that will not budge in me or out of me. I have been told to write by others (including religious) but what can I write? I know nothing – I am nothing but a "pain" that is lost in my doing and I feel lost forever.

"… This state of soul continues as days, weeks, months and years pass, though it does vary in intensity. Sometimes it lightens up little by little, and other times it becomes unbearable. I am surprised I can continue living. I Am, I love You and You love me. I know I want nothing but You – my Everything. I know the "absence of You" is You. I feel united to You – in pain – in this darkness.

"My faith tells me this. These are not just 'words' for me. It is You. In my pain I am possessed by You. I believe this! I must believe this! I have no other choice or place to run. You, my God – my only Family. Beauty, Light, that is darkness to me, and that is slowly putting me to death, but also sustains me. I die but I live. It is a pain that is unbearable, but I want it – I desire it with an insanity.

"It is weird – When I do not live "it" I miss it. Why? Because something tells me that there in my loneliness, You are accompanying me. We are together – suffering. You are lost in me and I in You. Where is this "place?" My faith tells me that this place is You…. Well, my "Silence" that speaks to me, but which also puts me to death and yet which sustains me – I lay down with You and You with me..."

Throughout this time, I was able to minister, teach and do my daily chores. I could play table tennis, but within I felt like a "tomb" and the community believed I was fine. St.

John of the Cross's writings were immensely helpful during this time, along with a contemporary author named Barbara Dent who wrote, *My Only Friend Is Darkness: Living the Night of Faith with St. John of the Cross*. In what direction could I go? My spiritual director had returned to the United States. It is not easy to find a good spiritual director. It is even more difficult to find a director who was experienced in such things, or who had themselves experienced this. At times I would meet a priest in Colombia, where I was giving retreats, who was known as the "Wise Man of Priests" and who is an excellent theologian, mystic and an exorcist.

This priest and I became friends and he was helpful, although I only saw him once a year. To a soul that is "thirsty," this "drop of water" provided refreshment and understanding grounded in a listening borne from years of experience, and from a way of life that is authentic. These annual meetings with this holy, elderly priest went a long way toward helping me persevere and "fight the good fight" along the way.

During the celebration of a Mass, as I was praying the Lord's prayer, I heard in my heart for the first time His voice since Mother Superior's leaving, and He said, "Lay down on the cross with me." This was the first sense of closeness I had felt with our Lord during the trial that had pressed so hard upon me. I had been told months ago by my spiritual director, "Do not waste this suffering." So, at the altar during Mass, I told Jesus, "I accept this suffering with my whole existence. FIAT!"

This change in my perspective made all the difference! Up to that moment the cry in my heart had been, "Why are you doing this to me?" I would shout that in my mind to her who had left. And in my prayers, I had been barely able to pronounce the name "Jesus."

All I could do was groan and moan before Him in the Blessed Sacrament! How often I had arguments with absent Mother Superior in my mind. Then I would realize how useless this was, and thinking of her not returning to the community was torturous at best. This was coupled with the thoughts from the Enemy that went like this: "You are a failure. Some religious community you have. Do you think you can heal the family? You are a fake, and it will be found out!" I felt powerless and defeated – sometimes feeling as if I just had to crumble underneath the weight of the burden and just cry.

However, I still had to focus on my community members and the so many poorest of the poor who also felt abandoned by her and who came to me for counseling and their many other needs. Only if you have lived among the poorest of the poor in a third-world country will you begin to understand the suffering within the hearts of the poor.

How do we pray at such moments? In Romans 8 we are told

> "that the Spirit too comes to the aid of our weakness; for we do not know how to pray as we ought."(Rom 8:26)

My groanings and tears became my prayer, though there was no consolation in sight. In my mind, I would go back and forth in just moments between "She will come to see and return to the community" and "No, she will never return." This constant back and forth proved both torturous and completely exhausting. I decided not to listen to either argument, and instead lay it before God and give this pain entirely to Him.

I began to see what I could not see before. When one is in a dark cave, one cannot even see his hand in front of his nose. This was me! But eventually the eyes adjust and one begins to see what before was not even a faint image. So too did this begin to happen within my soul. At first, all I saw was the darkness of not understanding the reasons for, and the pain of, her departure from the community. Later, however, I realized that this darkness was not due to Mother Superior's departure, but that I had entered the dark night of the soul.

Though this darkness was blacker than black, as more months passed, I began to see through the darkness a little, and then to sense our Lord's closeness. Though I still could not see God, I DID feel Him next to me on the cross – as a shadowy presence, a shadow cast by God himself.

Suffering was no longer my enemy, but become a mysterious companion – for there in my suffering I discovered my Jesus. My cross had become His cross. No longer did I groan, "Where are You?" but instead "Where are You not?" I began to see that God had a purpose – one that was about Him, and not about me.

And wonderfully, I realized eventually He was EVERYWHERE to be found! We are told in Psalm 139, "Darkness is not dark for you, and night shines as the day. Darkness and light are but one." (Ps 139:12) Then I found myself living, breathing in this truth – God Alone Suffices, as Saint and Doctor of the Church Teresa of Avila so famously wrote!!

So why do "bad things happen to good people," to people trying to do the "right thing" – God's will? This is a mystery only fully illuminated by the mystery of the Cross. In part, we know we are not good enough – we constantly put ourselves above our loving Father. We are told in Revelation 21:27 that "…nothing unclean will enter it [heaven]…" To share in the life (and it is beyond the wildest dreams of any of us) that is the trinitarian life, we must (due to our sins and attachments) be brought low, as a ball must hit bottom so that it can bounce high. This is St. John of the Cross. We think others, places, and things will fulfill us and give us what only God can give.

But you and I have an appetite for the Eternal – the Uncreated, God. We live under an illusion if we believe that people, places and things can really make us happy. Only God suffices! God ALONE!

When once upon a time I cursed the events and the suffering that God had allowed – my father- and mother-wounds, the kidnapping, the Mother Superior leaving and other events I choose not to discuss here, I now know and live for only Him (my Papa) and want to show and tell everyone that all this was necessary for a deeper encounter with my True FAMILY, the Blessed Trinity – Father, Son and Holy Spirit.

In *Making Sense Out of Suffering…*, " Peter Kreeft writes of suffering, "It is for your sake, not his [God's]. He's the joy that you've always wanted. Now your tears are your road to him, even when you think they're the reason for turning away from him. You can't escape. Not even into tears. He was there too." [48]

---

[48] Ibid. Pages 163-164.

Really God is found where we thought He was not – in our suffering on the cross. During the time I spent in my "dark night," I learned that a heart's suffering goes through a Holy Week.

> On Holy Thursday, the disciples scattered away from Jesus for fear of being caught up in events. A person living Holy Thursday goes to great lengths to avoid pain, to remain strong.

> On Good Friday, the disciples realized Jesus had been crucified and was dead. At this stage, the person living Good Friday begins to talk about their pain and loss, and gives themselves permission to cry and experience emotions. He does not attempt to avoid the cause and subject of the pain.

> Moving on to Holy Saturday, the disciples gathered together in a hidden place, and the promise of the Resurrection had not yet come to pass, nor had it been experienced. A person at this stage admits what has happened, has felt the pain and has begun to see and experience some of the fruits coming from their suffering. They are becoming more other-centered, that is, sensitive to others' suffering. Their suffering, also at this point, has led to a growth in their life of prayer and to greater generosity.

Finally, Easter Sunday arrives! The disciples are both overwhelmed and overjoyed by the truth of the resurrection. They experience a new type of freedom that overpowers them, inspiring them to proclaim the greatness of God and His victory on the Cross. A person living Easter Sunday experiences that he is overwhelmed by God, and no longer by the past painful event. He experiences, as I definitely experienced, a new freedom from the painful past, yet neither of us would trade off this suffering for anything – as it has brought us to experience what St Paul wrote in Romans 8:21 "…the glorious freedom of the children of God."

[For more detailed treatment of this viewpoint, please see applicable Appendix at end of this book.]

And we MUST share in His Holy Week, His suffering, if we are to share in His life as THE Son. There is no other way. There is no Easter Sunday without Good Friday. Notice the word before Friday – Good! Yes, all becomes somehow and in God's time "good." My dear reader, I do not know what you are going through, or where you are in your life.

Are you still living in the middle of the suffering and tragedies of Good Friday, or are you slowly moving to

Holy Saturday – when you are able to begin accepting what has happened and are begging to see the Father and His will for you? The Cross is a school and is learned in the heart. Sure, good books can help but ultimately it is a faith born out of the cross. Peter Kreeft, writing on how the life, death and resurrection have changed our suffering and tears, puts it beautifully,

> "For the darkest door of all has been shoved open and light from beyond it has streamed into our world to light our way, since he has changed the meaning of death. It is not merely that he rose from the dead, but that he changed the meaning of death, and therefore also of all the little deaths, all the sufferings that anticipate death and make up parts of it.
>
> "Death like cancer, seeps back into life. We lose little bits of life daily – our health, our strength, our youth, our hopes, our dreams, our friends, our children, our lives – all these dribble away like water through our desperate, shaking fingers.
>
> "Nothing we can do, not even our best efforts, holds our lives together. The only lives that don't spring leaks are the ones that are already watery. The only hearts that don't break are the ones that are busily constructing little hells of loveless control, cocoons

of safe, respectable selfishness to insulate themselves from the tidal waves of tears that come sooner or later...

"Henceforth, when we feel the hammers of life beating on our heads or on our hearts, we can know – we must know – that He is here with us taking our blows. Every tear we shed becomes his tear. He may not yet wipe it away, but He makes them His. Would we rather have our own dry eyes, or His tear-filled ones? He came. He is here. That is the salient fact." [49]

All things eventually are somehow the "Will of the Father" or allowed by Him. With time and through much pain and suffering, I have discovered the following truth:

O, Beloved of my life! You were right and I was wrong.
I shouted at you, "Where are you?"
Your silence was frightening.
I shouted louder and you whispered.
But I could not hear You or see You.
The truth was, You never left me.
You my Lord, faithful and so, so, good!
I am yours and you are mine. You are my All!
All is Necessary from your hand,

---

[49] Ibid. Pages 132-133.

And now I see it was because You loved me
As no one ever had or ever will.
You allowed what You allowed.
Blessed be God, for through all You allowed
You were there!
In All You are with me!
My soul now lives in this reality.
All is somehow good
For You are Goodness itself!

I KNOW this is what has happened. And it no longer matters what happens, for He is with me. As long as I do not lose Him, I am truly happy.

For happiness on earth is to live in Him, in His will!

Epilogue

Well, my dear brothers and sisters in God's family. Many years have passed since I began writing this book.

I look back at my life and this 'father wound,' and I am ever so grateful to God for it and everything else that He has allowed in the form of suffering. This wound and other difficulties that God has allowed make me know, really know, how much I have needed and will always need Him.

All He has allowed enabled me to discover that we all finally have a perfect family. A family with no dysfunction, no addiction, faithful and who loves us unconditionally – the Blessed Trinity!

This FAMILY wants to parent us all our lives, and has a divine purpose – to form us into sons and daughters in THE Son, Jesus. Considering that our True Home is in

Heaven, we truly are, as St. Peter writes, in exile here on earth.

Our life on earth is so very short when compared to Eternity. It is as but a drop of water compared to all the oceans, and other bodies of water combined on our planet. My wounds once affected my 'vision' or my apparent reality negatively. But through the healing process that drew me ever closer to God, He used my wounds to help me see true reality – to see God all around me.

Yes, God's plans for you and me are only for good. What goodness!!!!!

I pray this attempt to share my heart and some experience of my life and prayers have been helpful. Please KNOW you are not alone.

If your problems – your wounds – draw you God, then it is all good. If not, I will pray for you. We will meet face to face in heaven. My day for my homecoming is approaching a day at a time. I look forward to going home soon, and to seeing you there in His timing.

May you be held in Papa's eternal and loving embrace and you realize more and more that you are His, and He is yours!

In the name of the Father, the Son and the Holy Spirit, Amen.

Fr. Philip

If anyone wants to contact me to schedule a retreat, parish mission or conference speaker/presenter, please email me at padre.felipe.scott@gmail.com.

Appendices

SOME WORDS FOR THOSE DISCERNING WHETHER OR NOT TO HAVE CHILDREN

You might be thinking, "But I am afraid of how many I will have and if we can handle this." Yes, we must be responsible and prayerful in our parenting. That is why the Church allows the use of NFP (Natural Family Planning) for serious reasons. God wants to fulfill His plan. But we must look for Him in every area of our family life.

After working with families and founding a community of priests, brothers and sisters to heal the family I must tell you that sex and abstinence is not the problem that breaks up families. I humbly tell you that we (whether married or not) must learn to really love and know those with whom we are called to share a life-long commitment – whether it be through the sacrament of marriage or celibacy.

Ultimately, what is at stake is to learn to love – whether it be as a married person or as a celibate. The Catholic teaching on family planning gives couples the "space and choices" to learn to get close in a non-genital way. If you say "Yes" to God's Wisdom in such periods of abstinence you will love in a way where you will see and feel a passion that comes from the soul. You will discover a closeness that is closer than bodies can reach. As a priest I know this to be true. I know this closeness; this being known and knowing someone in a way that does not lead to the bedroom but to God.

I am not saying that couples who celebrate the marital act do not experience God. I **am** emphasizing the need for couples to learn and experience an intimacy that is experienced in a non-genital way.

These are not just words. So many couples I have counseled have a lot of sex but have never really known and noticed each other. We were meant to be known by another who loves us. Many couples experience a deep and quiet loneliness though they sleep in the same bed together for many years. This can be seen when I see an older couple at a restaurant. They are sitting in front of each other with nothing to say to one another. They cannot even look into each other's eyes.

I have often seen couples on my retreats during a meditation where I have them look into each other's eyes and stay there for five or ten minutes. I lead them to realize that God is there with them. Yes, He is there when they celebrate the marital act, but He wants to lead them to a deeper love, a love that is non-tangible. Soon I see couples fall into each other's arms crying, their souls having touched each other. At times it has been described to me in this way – "I felt that God in my husband [or my wife, as the case may be] was looking at God in me."

Usually, this experience opens them to a new way of being touched. It is as real as when they celebrate the marital act. Yet I believe it is more hidden – more mysterious. Many couples tell me they felt as if God was beholding them as they looked into each other's eyes. They experience being watched by God in a way that was very healing. They really tasted that their love was not just between them but which included God as the center of their relationship.

It is also important to remember that any appetite which is enjoyed can lose its impact and its ability to really satisfy. For example, if someone has a candy bar every day, he will not enjoy it as much as if they had one once a week. In the community we choose to enjoy sweets only on Sundays when it is not the liturgical season of Lent or Advent. So, when one of us returns from the US with a new batch of American candy, there is joy upon seeing the new arrival of sweets from abroad. We even laugh while eating a chocolate on such days. It is a joyful experience.

So too when I have discussed with couples this appetite and gift of God in their married life, those that for serious reasons choose to avoid a pregnancy,[50] and enter into a period of abstinence, when they return to give themselves to one another in the marital act, they found they enjoyed each other in a deeper and more profound way. They speak of the gift of their marital act as "True Gift," in a way and with words that show reverence. They look at each other in a way that mysteriously touches on how the Godly is somehow involved in the marital act. It is a beautiful experience for me to hear and see couples share with such vulnerability the sacredness of the marital embrace.

I must tell you that when I see and hear a couple share and discuss the same topic, but who are not faithful to the Church's teaching, they often reveal that it has become rote. The wife is usually the one that admits this fact. When I hear a wife share her heart, it is often filled with pain. All the sex has not really brought them closer, and you can see a distance, a wall between them. Often, sex

---

[50] Please see again Chapter 1, paragraph 4, sub-paragraph "A word on birth control and contraception" for a refresher of my previous discussion on this topic.

is used as a way to "deal" with deeper issues. It is their "fix-it kit." The issues do not go away.

As a priest, the best way I can explain is to describe the tone and words used by couples who practice the Church's teaching on birth control and those who do not is this:

> When I hold a chalice with the Precious Blood of Christ, I do it in way and use a language that communicates the unique moment of the consecration. It is quite a different experience to hold a glass of Coke. The Precious Blood of Christ is another reality, a Presence in this world but which is not of this world. Often, I have counseled couples who have different, sometimes hugely different, perspectives and experiences of the marital act. They talk about the same things but in a quite different way, and see them through different lenses.

What does the Church's teaching about the marital act teach couples about God's will in their lives and in the lives of their children? Living out God's will in our daily lives, especially where we are stretched beyond our strength, and yet responding to Him in faith and trust, allows us to speak to our children and others with an authority that will be noticed. They will notice that there is a sacrificial cost to do God's will. For example, if we were to hear testimony of a person who was in a Nazi concentration camp, it would sound different and impact an audience differently than if we heard a person talk on the same topic who had only "book" knowledge on the topic.

So, it is with a couple who has felt the pain of trusting in God's wisdom, and who shares and discusses the topic of being open to God's will in all matters – as opposed to those who pick and choose the areas in which they will be open to God's will. The trusting couple truly has "been there" and "all in" with the Lord. As this couple wrestles with trusting God beyond their limits of stress and understanding, they are assured by God that He will care for those who do His will. As the Lord says through the prophet Malachi,

> "try me in this, says the LORD of hosts: Shall I not open for you the floodgates of heaven, to pour down blessing upon you without measure?"(Mal 3:10)

That is what is experienced when we choose God's will. We experience God's fidelity to our sometimes fragile yesses to His will. Heaven opens, even when at first the gates seem to be closed because His will is difficult and it leads us to "cry out" to Him.

Yet, God's will eventually leads us to a peace beyond our human understanding.

Why is it so difficult to trust? Likely because we have experienced hurtful human betrayal. But our Father is not like that – He is ALWAYS faithful. His will and wisdom are theological, which literally means "God-logic." A life of fidelity and seeking His "will on earth as it is in heaven" prepares us to see and receive God's insight and His peace – not as the world gives peace. In John 14:27, we read "Peace I leave with you; my peace I give to you. Not as the world gives do I give it to you. Do not your hearts be troubled or afraid."

It is a peace that comes from "living" in God's will in such a way that it no longer matters what, where or when He is asking. To "live" this is to taste what St. Paul wrote in his letter to the Galatians, "... yet I live, no longer I, but Christ lives in me..." (Gal 2:20)

Christ did whatever the Father wanted. Period!

That is the challenge to which the Church's teaching opens a couple – doing God's will, even if it will be difficult. Period!

A HEART'S SUFFERING THROUGH ITS PERSONAL HOLY WEEK

Expounding on a Heart's Holy Thursday - Easter Sunday Ceasing to Suffer Incorrectly, and Learning to Suffer Correctly

Let's review more in depth the concept of a heart suffering through its own Holy Week, a concept I introduced in Chapter 10. Learning how to suffer correctly and how to cease to suffer incorrectly is such a gift, and one the Lord wants so much to give to you.

My suffering due to Mother Superior's departure catapulted me into an extended period of living the dark night of the soul. One of the fruits that came from that dark night was that I was taught the general process that a person goes through to heal. Today I see that I was taught how to suffer correctly and how to cease to suffer incorrectly.

Though I was in total darkness, my heart was taking notes and it was being given an understanding of how to suffer correctly on this side of eternity. This is one of life's most important lessons while we live on earth. I understood that the human heart goes through a personal Holy Week – and that this process includes a Holy Thursday, a Good Friday, a Holy Saturday and an Easter Sunday.

Holy Thursday

The disciples fled when Jesus was arrested and taken from their midst. So too, on one's personal Holy Thursday a person flees and avoids his pain at all costs. They avoid their pain and what caused their suffering in many ways. They do not talk about or feel their pain, and instead numb the pain by becoming hyperactive or a workaholic, or by pursuing a lifestyle of addictions – all the while acting as if not feeling means being strong. As a result of this numbness, they are not capable of being emotionally close to someone – even themselves. The majority of the world is stuck in this stage of the process. They don't know how to suffer, and being not connected to their pain, they become deformed by it. They don't know who they are and their pain dictates their choices, words and even identity. For instance, I have met many who struggle with sexual identity and ministered to them, and they all have terrible wounds that have never healed.

True story…in 1995 I was in Seoul, South Korea, teaching in front of over 4,000 at a Jesuit university, and I received a "word of knowledge" during a healing service when our Lord was exposed in the Blessed Sacrament. This is what Jesus said to me in my heart, "There are women here who were sex slaves of the Japanese. I want to heal them." I shared the word of knowledge in English and my translator repeated it in Korean.

Immediately the whole auditorium was filled with the cry of heart-wrenching pain expressed by these poor women that were once sex slaves. I have never heard such wailing. Their cries came from the depths of their souls, and continued non-stop for 15 minutes. Up to that moment these poor women had lived and were stuck in the Holy Thursday of suffering. They had tried to avoid their pain, and be strong in living with this secret agony.

Our Lord said "Enough!" This is what must happen if we are to heal. Our wounds must be opened up by Our Lord and we take this opportunity to feel, cry and talk about our pain. Now we begin to enter the Good Friday.

Good Friday

During Good Friday, the disciples could not run from the fact that Our Lord had been imprisoned, tortured, crucified and was now dead. No amount of imagination or avoidance could change this fact. Jesus was dead. He had been killed on the cross. So too, in this stage of the process of suffering people choose to stop avoiding the existence of their pain.

They must face the pain of their lives, allow themselves to feel their pain and talk about what happened. At first the pain of their suffering might cause them to cry out "Where are you God?" Such pain at first blinds them, because all they experience is suffering and they are even tempted to believe that their suffering will never cease.

That is not true. The human heart has seasons. There is a winter, there is a fall, there is a spring and there is a summer. We have to respect the "laws" of our human heart. It is important to remind ourselves during this Good Friday that it too will pass. For the moment "I feel this way," but that is not the whole truth. How long this "Good Friday" lasts depends on the type of wound and how deep the healing needs to go. What is necessary in this stage is that I stop trying to be "strong" and allow myself to "hit my rock bottom."

Suffering is a tool used by God to do a deep work in the heart of a person – necessary work. Yes, suffering is necessary if we are to share in the glory (in the beauty) of God. St. Paul in Romans 8:17 writes "…if only we suffer with him so that we may also be glorified with him." So, to share in the beauty of God - his glory, we must also share in the suffering of Jesus.

Suffering can free us from sinful habits. In 1 Peter 4:1, we read "Therefore since Christ suffered in the flesh, arm yourselves also with the same attitude (for whoever suffers in the flesh has broken with sin…)." During my suffering that lasted so exceedingly long, it was on my personal Good Friday that I began to see that good things were happening.

For example, I was becoming more sensitive to the pain of others. My daily prayer life doubled. My regrettable anger issue was radically declining. I was less judgmental. I had grown in gentleness and was prone to listen more to others before I responded. I was realizing that what God had allowed and was allowing was necessary for a deeper conversion and purification in my life. Eventually, I found myself moving on to Holy Saturday.

Holy Saturday

During this stage one sees positive fruits brought about through suffering, yet the suffering has not ended. Rather, it becomes long-suffering and one asks themselves, "How much longer do I need to suffer? When will it end?" In this stage one is tempted to "throw in the towel," to stop praying because Holy Saturday might last the longest. One has not yet seen and does not yet understand the full reason for their suffering. They sense the finish line ahead, but know it is still in the distance. They want it over…

Yet they realize that it was good the suffering occurred. We are impatient creatures! The devil does not want us to understand that suffering can be one of the greatest gifts that God allows in our lives. Suffering seems to cause death, but the Truth is that suffering is full of life, Divine Life – or as Jesus said in John 10:10, "that they might have life and have it more abundantly." Suffering also is God's way to teach us that he is truly with us. That He is Emmanuel, God with us. We are told in Isaiah 30:20 (RSV), "And though the Lord give you the bread of adversity and the water of affliction, yet your Teacher will not hide himself…"

One receives a new interior sensitivity to see and experience God's presence and the activity of the Holy Spirit. One senses God's approaching footsteps and one's heart is opened up to His silent voice. So, suffering bears the fruit of a new openness to God's ever active presence who is, as St Thomas Aquinas said, "pure act."

Easter Sunday

Those who have reached the Easter Sunday in the process of suffering no longer cry out, "Where are you God?" Rather, we now ask Him "Where are you not?" We experience what St Paul says in Romans 8:21 "the glorious freedom of children of God." We don't regret what happened that brought us to our terrible dark night. We wouldn't change one detail.

No, we might not want to go through it again, but now we truly see. Where once suffering blinded us, suffering now has truly taught us to see in a new way. As the cross gave us our greatest gift of salvation, so suffering "our cross" has birthed in us like never before a "living God." This is what I experienced after my time of utter darkness was past.

During this event of suffering and darkness God delivered me from the issue of anger, my deep emotional and spiritual wound, as well as my mother wound, and I was brought to a new, profound and satisfying intimacy with God.

EVEN (ESPECIALLY) WHEN WE BLOW IT ROYALLY, GOD IS STILL FAITHFUL

I love German Shepherds! In fact, my twin says that I love them so much that I smell people before I greet them. Once, I had a German Shepherd named Max, who was a very, very good dog. He was very well-trained, including obedience and protection training. Max was with me like white on rice, and we were inseparable.

Down the street from where we were renting a house in Peru, there was a gentleman who raised champion German Shepherds. Because of our common love for German Shepherds, we became friends, and often talked about our dogs. Eventually, I realized he had financial needs and that he had supposedly suffered because of a company who was on the front pages of the newspaper for committing various injustices against him and others of its employees.

The story remained in the headlines for weeks. I felt terrible about his predicament and would help him financially so he would not end up on the streets with his wife and children. He would tell me his emergency needs, and I would open up the wallet of my community to meet his needs. My community expressed their distrust of him, and even my Max would growl at him whenever Max saw the man. In his own way, Max tried to tell me not to trust this man, but I knew better…

After all, this man loved German Shepherds - how could I not trust him? The man had to be good, right? For over a year we helped him, and for over a year my community told me again and again, "I don't think you should trust him." Even my dog growled for over a year! To make a long painful story short, the gentleman was lying to us, and he swindled my community out of $50,000! I was beyond furious – both at the man and myself! I thought I knew better, and I should have known better. My community tried to warn me, and so did my dog, but NO, I knew better.

When I realized the man had been lying to me, I wanted to reform his face with my fists. I asked my community's forgiveness for not listening to them. Yes, God tried repeatedly to warn me through my community and my dog. But I was too proud to listen to them or to Max.

The pain of this experience was worsened much more considering that my community was also building our house during this time, and the foreman of the construction crew told me, "Father, we need $50,000 within two weeks to finish building the house." Where was the $50,000? I was furious, but even more, my pride was hurt. I thought I knew better, but NO I most certainly did not!

Going to Jesus in the tabernacle, I stuck my head in it and I said to Him, "What do I do? My community told me not to trust him, and even Max tried to tell me. I need $50,000 in two weeks. What do I do?" Then, a peace came upon me, and I heard the words "Call XX and X in the United States and tell them what happened – but do not ask them for a penny."

I obeyed and did just that. Within two weeks we received $65,000! You might ask, "why $65,000? Your community needed only $50,000."

Well, when the foreman went to purchase the building materials to finish construction, the prices had gone up $15,000! God took care of the inflation when I was not even considering that! God knew everything! Papa is So SO good!

Even in my sin and pride and stubbornness, He remains faithful!

Bibliography

BOOKS

Biela, Slawomir. (2002). *God Alone Suffices*. Ventura, CA: In the Arms of Mary Foundation. (Hardcover)

Brother Lawrence. (2019). *The Practice of the Presence of God*. India, New Delhi, Daryaganj: General Press. (Hardcover)

De Montfort, St. Louis. (1941). *True Devotion to Mary with Preparation for Total Consecration*. France: Fathers of the Company of Mary. Retypeset in 2010 by Gastonia, NC: TAN Books, and published with assistance of The Livingstone Corporation. (Paperback)

Dent, Barbara. (1988). *My Only Friend is Darkness: Living the Night of Faith with St. John of the Cross*. Norte Dame, IN: Ave Maria Press. (Hardcover)

Hardon, John. (1985). *Pocket Catholic Dictionary*. New York, NY: Doubleday, a division of Bantam Doubleday Dell Publishing Group, Inc. (Paperback)

Kreeft, Peter. (1986). *Making Sense Out of Suffering*. Cincinnati, OH: Servant, an imprint of Franciscan Media. (Paperback)

Philippe, Father Jacques. (2007). *In the School of the Holy Spirit*. Strongsville, OH: Scepter Publishers.

Ratzinger, Joseph (Pope Benedict XVI). (2007). *Jesus of Nazareth*. Vatican City: Liberia Editrice Vaticana (original publisher); published in the United States – New York, NY: Doubleday, an imprint of the Broadway Publishing Group, a division of Random House Inc. (Paperback) [This is the first-published volume in Pope Benedict's trilogy on the life of Jesus.]

Schwarzkopf, General Norman. (1992). *It Doesn't Take a Hero*. New York, NY: Bantam Books, a division of Bantam Doubleday Dell Publishing Group Inc.

Smalley, Gary and Trent, John. (1986). *The Blessing*. New York NY: Pocket Books, a division of Simon & Schuster, Inc. (Paperback)

Stoop, David. (2004). *Making Peace with Your Father*. Ventura, CA: Regal Books from Gospel Light. (Paperback)

CDs

McDonald, Deacon Bob. (date unknown). *Anger and Forgiveness.* Lighthouse Catholic Media/Augustine Institute. [Can be ordered from the catholic.market website.]

PSYCHIATRIC STUDY

He J, Yan X, Wang R, Zhao J, Liu J, Zhou C, Zeng Y. *Does Childhood Adversity Lead to Drug Addiction in Adulthood? A Study of Serial Mediators Based on Resilience and Depression.* Front Psychiatry. 2022 Apr 18

Biographical Summary – Father Philip Scott

Fr. Philip Scott was born in Lima, Peru and is a priest of the diocese of Saint Petersburg in Florida. In 1998, Father founded the community of Family of Jesus in Lima, Peru.

He has served God and the Body of Christ as a priest for over 35 years, and is a graduate of Mount St. Mary's Seminary in Emmitsburg, MD.

He is a retreat master who gives retreats within the United States and worldwide in both Spanish and English to lay people, youth, couples and priests.

Fr. Philip has been featured on EWTN's Women of Grace, Living His Life Abundantly, Pepe Alonso's EWTN program Nuestra Fe En Vivo and has also been speaker at apologetics conferences. Through this book, Father hopes to share healing and hope through God the Father!